HOW THINGS EXIST

LAMA ZOPA RINPOCHE

How Things Exist
TEACHINGS ON EMPTINESS

Edited by Ailsa Cameron

LAMA YESHE WISDOM ARCHIVE • BOSTON
www.LamaYeshe.com

A non-profit charitable organization for the benefit of all
sentient beings and an affiliate of the Foundation for
the Preservation of the Mahayana Tradition
www.fpmt.org

First published 2008
15,000 copies for free distribution

Lama Yeshe Wisdom Archive
PO Box 356
Weston
MA 02493, USA

Library of Congress Cataloging-in-Publication Data

Thubten Zopa, Rinpoche, 1945-
How things exist : teachings on emptiness / Lama Zopa Rinpoche ;
edited by Ailsa Cameron.
p. cm.
Summary: "This book begins with a general talk on universal responsibility and compassion that is followed by four chapters detailing the
Prasangika Madhyamaka view of emptiness, or ultimate reality, as taught
in the Gelug tradition of Tibetan Buddhism, and how to meditate on it,
according to the author's personal experience"—Provided by publisher.
Includes bibliographical references.
ISBN 978-1-891868-20-7 (alk. paper)
1. Dge-lugs-pa (Sect)—Doctrines. 2. Prasangika. 3. Lam-rim. I. Cameron,
Ailsa. II. Title.
BQ7640.T49 2008
294.3'420423—dc22
                                                        2007048611

10 9 8 7 6 5 4 3 2 1

Cover photograph by John Berthold, courtesy Wisdom Publications
Cover line art by Robert Beer • Interior photographs of Rinpoche at Yucca
Valley, CA, 1977, by Carol Royce-Wilder • Designed by Gopa & Ted2 Inc.

♻ Printed in the USA with environmental mindfulness on 50% PCW
recycled paper. The following resources have been saved: 39 trees,
1,812 lbs. of solid waste, 14,108 gallons of water, 3,399 lbs. of greenhouse
gases and 27 million BTUs of energy.

Please contact the Lama Yeshe Wisdom Archive for more copies of this
and our other free books

···Contents···

··· Publisher's Acknowledgments ···

WE ARE EXTREMELY GRATEFUL to our friends and supporters who have made it possible for the LAMA YESHE WIS-
DOM ARCHIVE to both exist and function: to Lama Yeshe and Lama
Zopa Rinpoche, whose kindness is impossible to repay; to Peter and
Nicole Kedge and Venerable Ailsa Cameron for their initial work on
the ARCHIVE; to Venerable Roger Kunsang, Lama Zopa's tireless
assistant, for his kindness and consideration; and to our sustaining
supporters: Barry & Connie Hershey, Joan Halsall, Roger & Claire
Ash-Wheeler, Claire Atkins, Thubten Yeshe, Richard Gere, Doren
& Mary Harper, Tom & Suzanne Castles, Lily Chang Wu and Hawk
Furman.

We are also deeply grateful to all those who have become members
of the ARCHIVE over the past few years. Details of our membership
program may be found at the back of this book, and if you are not a
member, please do consider joining up. Due to the kindness of those
who have, we now have three editors working on our vast collection
of teachings for the benefit of all. We have posted our list of indi-
vidual and corporate members on our Web site, www.LamaYeshe.
com. We also thank Henry & Catherine Lau and S. S. Lim for their
help with our membership program in Singapore and Serina Yap for

her help with our membership program in Malaysia. Thank you all so much for your foresight and kindness.

In particular, we thank Ven. Ailsa Cameron for her decades of meticulous editing in general and her wonderful editing of the teachings in this book in particular, and also those who specifically contributed to its publication: Wee Sin Tho, Henry Lau, Sonal Shastri and an anonymous Australian benefactor.

Furthermore, we would like to express our appreciation for the kindness and compassion of all those other generous benefactors who have contributed funds to our work since we began publishing free books. Thankfully, you are too numerous to mention individually in this book, but we value highly each and every donation made to spreading the Dharma for the sake of the kind mother sentient beings and now pay tribute to you all on our Web site. Thank you so much.

Finally, I would like to thank the many other kind people who have asked that their donations be kept anonymous; my wife, Wendy Cook, for her constant help and support; our dedicated office staff, Jennifer Barlow and Sonal Shastri; Ven. Thubten Labdron (Trisha Donnelly) for her help with archiving and editing; Ven. Bob Alcorn for his incredible work on our Lama Yeshe DVDs; David Zinn for his digital imaging expertise; Veronica Kaczmarowski, Evelyn Williames, FPMT Australia and Mandala Books (Brisbane), for much appreciated assistance with our distribution in Australia; Dennis Heslop, Philip Bradley, Mike Gilmore and our other friends at Wisdom Books (London) for their great help with our distribution in Europe; our volunteer transcribers; and Greg Sneddon, Dr. Su Hung and Anne Pottage in Australia and Jonathan Steyn in London for their help with our audio work.

If you, dear reader, would like to join this noble group of open-hearted altruists by contributing to the production of more books by Lama Yeshe or Lama Zopa Rinpoche or to any other aspect of the Lama Yeshe Wisdom Archive's work, please contact us to find out how.

—Dr. Nicholas Ribush

Through the merit of having contributed to the spread of the Buddha's teachings for the sake of all sentient beings, may our benefactors and their families and friends have long and healthy lives, all happiness, and may all their Dharma wishes be instantly fulfilled.

· · · · ·

··· Editor's Preface ···

THIS BOOK IS a collection of five talks given by Lama Zopa Rinpoche in New York in 1990. The first two talks,[1] given at Columbia University on September 6 and 7, were public talks aimed at a general audience. In the first talk, Rinpoche focuses on the importance and power of compassion, with special emphasis on how each of us has universal responsibility, responsibility for the peace and happiness not just of the people and animals around us but of all living beings, who are just like us in wanting happiness and not wanting even the slightest suffering.

In the second talk, in the process of giving the oral transmission of a prayer outlining the graduated path to enlightenment, Rinpoche describes the nature of the enlightened state, the different types of happiness we can bring others, the nature of the mind and how the mind exists through a process of labeling. Rinpoche then gives a detailed explanation of how a table exists. (In another teaching, Rinpoche explains that he uses the example of a table so many times in his teachings on emptiness because it is usually the object directly in front of him.) Rinpoche then comes to the explanation of how the

[1] Lama Yeshe Wisdom Archive number 655

I exists, the most important point to understand. To conclude the talk, Rinpoche finally gives the oral transmission of the prayer, as well as the oral transmissions of various mantras. As the talks were titled "Transforming Problems," a subject he didn't directly address, Rinpoche then refers the audience to relevant books on thought transformation.

The remaining three talks,[2] given at the Great Enlightenment Temple, in the Bronx, on September 8 and 9 and aimed at a more Buddhist audience, focus mainly on the subject of emptiness. The first talk, after a preliminary meditation on impermanence and emptiness, once again addresses the need for compassion, the types of happiness that can be experienced, and the paths to that happiness. For the rest of the talks, Rinpoche concentrates on emptiness, especially emphasizing how things exist through a process of labeling a base and identifying the ignorance that is the root of all our sufferings, the concept of true existence. Rinpoche uses many examples, including the temple and its atoms, to illustrate his point. Rinpoche also describes various simple meditations on emptiness, as well as how to implement the understanding of emptiness in everyday life, especially in situations where there is a danger of harming ourselves and others.

Rinpoche concludes both sets of talks by reiterating that everything, including our happiness and suffering, comes from our own mind. As Rinpoche says at the end of Chapter 2: "The concept of a truly existent I, of an I having existence from its own side, is the very

[2] Lama Yeshe Wisdom Archive number 791

root of all problems, all suffering. In order to escape suffering, we need to eliminate this root, and for that reason we need to understand the emptiness, the ultimate nature, of the I. That is the essence of this talk." With simple immediate examples and a minimum of technical philosophical terms, Rinpoche explains very clearly how things—including, most importantly, the I—exist.

With thanks to Claire Atkins for her generous support, to Ven. Lhagsam for providing me with a room of my own, to Ven. Dekyong for her help with research, to the organizers of these talks, to Gareth Robinson and Segen Speer-Senner for transcribing the Columbia University talks and Nick Ribush, Wendy Cook and Jennifer Barlow for their editorial suggestions.

· · · 1 · · ·

Universal Responsibility

Firstst I would like to say thank you very much. I'm very happy to meet all of you, my brothers and sisters. At this time we are meeting each other to share something about our precious human qualities with respect to obtaining the real peace of mind and happiness that we need.

Because I haven't studied properly, I don't know much about Buddhism—what I know is like a drop of water from an ocean. But during this time that we have with each other, I'm happy to speak about and share the little that I have learned and tried to practice.

However, before the actual discourse, I'm going to recite the mantra of the kind, compassionate Shakyamuni Buddha.

[Rinpoche recites the *Praise to Shakyamuni Buddha* and Shakyamuni Buddha's mantra, TADYATHA OM MUNÉ MUNÉ MAHA MUNAYE SVAHA.]

The power of compassion

All beings, from humans down to the tiniest creatures that can be seen only through a microscope, are exactly the same in wanting happiness and not wanting suffering, or problems. It doesn't matter whether we are from the East, the West or another planet—we are exactly the same in this. It is for this reason that practice of the good heart, compassion, is the most important thing in our everyday life.

First of all, no matter how many friends we have—hundreds, or even thousands—if we don't have a warm, kind heart, we'll have no satisfaction or peace of mind in our everyday life. Since we need friends, we also need to develop our mind, especially our compassion. Compassion, which is the essence of the right path, brings the greatest benefit to all other beings and ourselves.

Without compassion, even if we find a friend, that friend can become our enemy. It depends on our attitude in everyday life, on whether our mind is compassionate in nature or self-centered, thinking about nothing but ourselves and our own happiness day and night.

If we have compassion, we have better, more harmonious relationships and more peace. With compassion, everyone becomes our friend. Wherever we go and whoever we live with, everyone becomes our friend. We find friends everywhere. If we have compassion, even someone who is normally cruel and selfish is kind to us. That's a result of our compassion. It is a common experience that even someone who is normally mean to others is kind to a person who is warm-hearted, who is kind, loving, and compassionate, with much concern for others.

Take my teacher, Lama Yeshe, for example. Many people here knew or know about Lama Yeshe. Those of you who didn't meet him might have heard about him. Lama Yeshe saw everyone as very kind.

From my observation, because of Lama's own good heart, other people also became kind and good-hearted. The other person's mind was also transformed or, in other words, blessed. *Blessed* means their mind was transformed from a negative attitude into a positive one, from a selfish, cruel mind into a kind mind.

Another example is the famous Italian saint, St. Francis of Assisi. I think St. Francis lived at the same time as the great Tibetan yogi, Milarepa, who achieved full enlightenment within a few years by meditating in hermitages in the Himalayas following the instructions of his guru, Marpa.

In a forest in Italy there lived a dangerous wolf that had harmed and killed many people. St. Francis told the local people, "Don't worry about this wolf. I'll go into the forest and ask him not to harm anyone."

The people begged St. Francis not to go into the forest because the wolf would attack him, but he went anyway. When the wolf saw St. Francis, it immediately became subdued. It was completely transformed, or blessed. Instead of attacking St. Francis, the wolf

licked his feet. It behaved the way a dog does with its master, showing humility and affection.

St. Francis then told the wolf, "Don't harm people. I'll beg for food
in the city and give it to you." From that day on, the wolf stopped
attacking people. St. Francis begged for food in the streets and fed
the wolf.

There are many other such stories of human beings who were
exactly the same as we are, with all the problems that we have, but
who put effort into developing their mind and were able to train
their mind in compassion for all beings. Shakyamuni Buddha and
all the buddhas of the three times, as well as all the great saints in
the various religions, were originally like us. They had ignorance,
anger, desire, jealousy, pride, ill will and all the other mental faults,
as well as all the other problems in life, but they didn't just leave
their life immersed in problems. They became different from us by
putting effort into developing their inner qualities, the qualities of
their mind. They reduced the faults of the mind and put effort into
developing its good qualities, the essence of which is compassion
for all beings.

If we have compassion in our heart, everyone becomes our
friend—even someone who is cruel to other beings, and even poi-
sonous snakes, tigers and other wild animals. No matter how wild or
violent such beings are, they cannot harm us because of the power
of the positive attitude of our compassion. Because of our vibration,
the blessing of our positive mind, even their attitude changes for the
better and they stop giving harm to others as well.

In Lhasa, there were three great monasteries—Sera, Ganden, and

Drepung[3]—which were like universities, except they didn't have the vast range of subjects that Western universities have but concentrated on the study and practice of the whole of Buddha's teachings. While study of the philosophy of other religions, particularly Indian ones, was included, the monks studied mainly the teachings of the Buddha. Furthermore, study was combined with practice, for the development of the mind.

Sera Monastery has two colleges: Sera-je, to which I belong, and Sera-me. One of the abbots of Sera-je, who was very learned and well known in Tibet, was able to escape from Tibet to India. He had a cat. Now usually, when a cat sees a mouse, it will immediately attack it. That's how cats normally act. Even though this cat was killing mice before, once it came to stay with the abbot and he started taking care of it, its mind changed. Even when a mouse would run around the room, the cat would never chase it but just stayed where it was, relaxed.

This happens because a person's mental development can affect and transform the environment. It can stop negativities; it can transform a negative environment into a positive one and others' negative thoughts into compassionate ones. To understand how this can happen it's important to understand that the negativity or positivity of an environment doesn't come from its own side; it comes from the mind. Whether a place is negative or positive, harmful or beneficial to one's health, depends on the minds of the people who live there.

[3] These three great Tibetan monasteries have now been reestablished in south India, where the monks continue to concentrate on the study and practice of the Buddha's teachings.

The mind is like a baby

The mind of most of us ordinary beings is like a child, a baby, and needs to be taken care of like a baby. We can't listen to and do everything that our mind says, just as we can't listen to and do everything that a child says. Before acting on what a child says we have to analyze whether or not it's worthwhile. If it is, we can do it; if it's not, we don't. Since our mind is like a child, it's dangerous to do everything it says—doing so can destroy our life; instead of bringing peace and happiness, it can bring great harm to us and others. Therefore, using our own wisdom, we need to analyze the validity of what our mind tells us to see whether it's beneficial or harmful. With that wisdom we can then direct, or guide, our mind. In other words, we can then guide and protect ourselves.

Therefore, it's essential that we develop wisdom. If we don't develop wisdom, our life becomes confused because we can't discriminate between what is wrong and to be abandoned and what is right—beneficial for us and others—and to be practiced. So compassion is one thing that's very important in life; wisdom is another.

With respect to the different kinds of wisdom, developing that which understands the mind is the most important. Without this, there's no way that we can escape from problems and the causes of problems, which are not outside our mind but within it. In other words, of all the different types of education, education about the mind is the most important.

Compassion is the very essence

Another point I'd like to make is that no matter how wealthy we are, if we lack compassion, there's no peace or satisfaction in our life. Even if we came to own everything on earth, we'd still not be satisfied. Without developing our mind and practicing compassion, there's no way to find peace and satisfaction in our life. Just as we need wealth and other material things, we also need mental development.

Similarly, no matter how much fame or worldly power we have, without transforming our mind, without practicing compassion, again there's no peace or happiness in our daily life.

Also, no matter how much education we have, if the inner factor of developing our mind is missing, if the practice of compassion is missing, again there's no peace in our life. Even if we have learned every language and have every other kind of knowledge that exists in the world, even if we have memorized and can explain all the Buddha's teachings, all the sutras and tantras, if we have not transformed our mind, if we have not developed compassion for other beings, once more our life will be full of problems. We will still have anger and the dissatisfied minds of desire, pride, jealousy and all the other delusions; with more education, our inner problems can become even bigger than they were before.

Therefore we have to study our mind, its faults and its qualities, and develop it in a positive direction. However, even though there are many realizations that we can achieve, compassion is the most important one. Compassion is the very essence.

With compassion in our daily life, we experience much happiness.

We get up with great joy and go to work with a happy mind. We live with our family with a happy, satisfied mind. We go to bed with a happy, satisfied mind. Our mind is stable all the time. And not only is there peace in our own everyday life, but there is peace for everybody else as well. Others receive peace from us.

Practicing the good heart is more important than having friends, more important than money, much more important than fame and power. Practicing the good heart is more important than every other form of education.

Without practicing the good heart, there's neither peace nor satisfaction in our life. It isn't grounded; it has no stability. Compassion should be the first thing we think of when we get up in the morning. Compassion, which is our own mind, is a wish-granting jewel; compassion fulfills all our wishes. There's nothing more important in life than transforming our mind into compassion and then developing it. That's why meditation is so important. Meditation is the essential means by which we transform our mind into compassion and then develop it. And meditation is also the way we develop wisdom; true wisdom also has to be developed through meditation.

If we have compassion in our heart, everything we do will be done out of that attitude and we will therefore not harm others but only benefit them. Even if our husband, wife or the person with whom we live does not meditate or practice the good heart but has a selfish, cruel attitude and constantly criticizes us, since we don't harm that person, he or she has peace, the peace of not receiving harm from us. That absence of harm is peace.

If we ourselves don't have compassion but act out of anger, desire, jealousy and so forth, we'll retaliate to that person's negative actions and therefore they'll receive more harm and experience more suffering. But even if that person doesn't practice at all, doesn't do anything with their mind, if we practice the good heart, that person receives much benefit.

If our mind is strong and stable in the practice of the good heart, we can also gradually cause that other person's mind to become stable. The way our companion's life turns out depends on us, on our example; whether that person's life turns out to be peaceful or dissatisfied depends on our attitude. If our mind is stable and compassionate in nature we will put all our energy into developing the good heart, not only for our own peace and happiness but especially for the peace and happiness of other sentient beings. Even though our companion might have an unstable mind, one minute up, the next minute down, or might be very impatient or self-centered, if our own mind is stable in the practice of the good heart, with our example the other person's life can become better. They can develop a better attitude and better behavior and experience more peace in their life. They will cause less harm to themselves and others and bring more benefit to others. We can cause their life to become better—happier and more peaceful.

For example, there were two people in Tibet—one was an alcoholic, the other didn't drink. They both went to Lhasa, the largest city in Tibet. The alcoholic met a friend who didn't drink and eventually stopped drinking himself. The other, who didn't drink before, met a friend who was an alcoholic and finished up becoming an alcoholic.

Each of us definitely has responsibility for our environment. For example, you are responsible for the peace and happiness of your family, for how their lives are going to turn out. There are infinite sentient beings but here I am talking about a small number, just the few people in your immediate family. You are completely responsible for their lives, for their attitudes and the way they live, whether it's with a good heart or with a harmful mind. You definitely have this responsibility. If you have compassion you won't give harm to the rest of your family, so even if they don't practice from their side, there's peace. If there are ten other people in your family, even if you are the only one practicing compassion, since those ten people don't receive harm from you, you give them peace.

Now, there are millions of people in your country. If you, the one person, have compassion, since all those millions of people don't receive harm from you, you are giving them peace. This is your contribution to the peace of your country.

It's the same for the rest of the world. If you have compassion, all the billions of human beings in this world and all the other sentient beings in the ocean, on the ground and in the air don't receive harm from you. Their bodies and minds not receiving harm from you is peace that they're receiving from you. This is your contribution to world peace. This is a real, practical contribution to world peace that you can make at any time, day or night.

Benefiting others

When we have compassion, not only do we stop harming others but we try to help them as well. We try to free others from their problems.

For example, someone with cancer knows how much people who have cancer are suffering. Because they are aware of this, they have much compassion for other people with cancer. Similarly, a person with AIDS has much compassion for other people who have AIDS because they know what their lives are like. Someone who has cancer or AIDS, because of compassion, always wants to do something to help others with the same problem; they put special effort into counseling or helping in other ways. They especially concentrate on that. Their efforts are dedicated particularly to helping people with cancer or AIDS.

Besides not giving harm to others, someone with compassion wants to help them. If someone has compassion, they not only stop giving harm to others, but in addition they help to free them from suffering. They think, "How can I help? What can I do to pacify this person's physical or mental sufferings?" They put effort into helping the person have physical comfort and happiness and peace of mind. Someone with compassion does something to benefit others, physically and mentally.

One person with compassion brings peace and happiness to the person they live with or the members of their family and to the many millions of people in their country. Millions of people receive happiness from this one person who has compassion. Not only that, but all sentient beings, all human beings and all other beings, who want happiness and do not want suffering, receive help and happiness from this one person who has compassion. So, when you have compassion, everyone receives help, or benefit, from you.

If you, the one person, don't practice compassion, starting with the person you live with, all the rest of the sentient beings don't receive peace, which is the absence of harm, and don't receive help. Therefore, starting with your family, the happiness of all the human beings on this earth, as well as that of all other sentient beings, is dependent on you. Each of us is completely responsible for the happiness of every sentient being. It is completely in our own hands. Starting with the people in our family and extending to all the rest of the sentient beings, it is completely in our hands whether they have peace and happiness in their lives. Whether they receive benefit or harm is completely up to us.

Again, we can see from this that each of us has this universal responsibility.

Therefore, compassion becomes even more important. Before I was talking about only your happiness, but here I'm talking about the happiness of all human beings and all other living beings. For the numberless human beings, the numberless animals, and all the numberless other living beings not to receive harm and to receive peace and happiness, it becomes crucial that you, one person, develop your mind and practice compassion. Compassion is so important and so precious. Why is it so precious? Because not only will you have happiness and success, but every other being will also benefit. They will not receive harm, which is benefit. Therefore, the compassion that you, one person, generate is very precious.

Universal responsibility in daily life

Another point is that even in daily life, when our mind is loving and compassionate and we are happy, it also makes our environment happy. Our family is happy. There is a smile on our face, and we have a loving, compassionate vibration. Our conversation is also loving and compassionate in nature. When we talk, our words are sweet and good to hear. Since our words are loving and compassionate, they don't cause harm. Even our conversation helps others, causing them happiness and freeing them from problems. Even by smiling out of our positive attitude, we make the people around us at our office or home happy. The environment and the people around us are influenced by how we behave.

Whenever we're very impatient, self-centered or dissatisfied and thinking about nothing but our own problems, our mind is very tight and our external appearance also reflects that. We have a kind of dark, sad appearance and this makes our environment sad. It upsets the people around us and makes them unhappy as well. When our mind is like that we also talk differently. Our conversation doesn't make others happy or free them from problems; it's not loving or compassionate.

The conclusion is that the way we behave in our everyday life affects not only the people around us but even the dogs, birds and other animals as well. Their happiness and suffering depends on us. We are completely responsible for the happiness of the people and animals around us in our daily life.

This is the first point: we are responsible for the happiness of other sentient beings. It's very important to meditate on this again and again and to feel it in our everyday life. We have to bring it to mind over and over again. At home, at the office or in the street, if our mind follows the self-cherishing thought and thinks only about "me, me, me, I, I, I, my happiness, my problems," our heart is very tight. When we follow our selfish mind, we put ourselves in prison—not a physical prison but a mental one. At such times, our heart is tight. Even if we try to relax physically, our mind is neither relaxed nor tranquil.

With this selfish attitude, even if we're eating food that costs thousands of dollars, we don't enjoy its taste. Even if we're wearing clothes that cost thousands of dollars, our mind is very dissatisfied, and we don't enjoy them. Even if we live in a palace built of gold, diamonds and other jewels, with every comfort available on this earth, since our mind is under the control of the self-cherishing thought, we have no peace or happiness. When our mind is under the control of egoism, there's no peace, happiness or enjoyment.

The stronger our selfish mind, the easier it is for us to get angry; our anger arises more strongly and quickly. Our dissatisfied mind of desire is also much stronger; jealousy arises more easily and strongly; all other problems arise more easily and strongly. The self-cherishing thought constantly tortures us and allows us no peace whatsoever.

However, when we live our life with the positive attitude of loving compassion, caring for and cherishing others, even if there's only water to drink, we're happy and enjoy it. Even if we live in just a simple stone house or a grass hut, there's much peace and enjoyment in our life. At work, at home with our family or simply walking down the street, when we change our attitude and think, "My life is not for me but for other sentient beings; my life is for other people, to pacify their sufferings and bring them happiness; this is the purpose of my life," we're immediately released from tension. When we change our attitude from self-cherishing to cherishing others, we immediately feel a big release from the tension in our heart. We're suddenly freed from the prison of self-cherishing. Suddenly there's relaxation and freedom in our life. Suddenly we find enjoyment and satisfaction. We see meaning in life, a purpose in living. With this attitude, we have much enjoyment. We enjoy looking at people. Nothing upsets or hurts us. With this attitude, we can look at people and feel close to them. Even if we don't know them, mentally, this is what happens. They become close to our heart. There's a positive feeling and a positive environment at home and at work. We see that happiness and suffering don't come from outside but from our own mind.

The second point I want to emphasize is the importance of remembering universal responsibility in daily life. When you get up in the morning, think, "I'm responsible for bringing happiness to all sentient beings and for pacifying all their sufferings and causes of suffering, which are in their mind." Even though there are many meditations, practices and other things you can do in our life, the most important thing you can do is to practice compassion. Practicing compassion is the most beneficial thing you can do for the happiness of other sentient beings, not to mention your own.

Then think, "My life is not for my own happiness. My life is for other sentient beings, to pacify all their sufferings and bring them all happiness. This is the purpose of my life. This is the reason that I have this precious human body."

Then, as you dress, think, "To do this work for other sentient beings, I need to be healthy and have a long life. Therefore, I'm putting on these clothes." It's as if you are taking care of a servant, the servant of all sentient beings, and this becomes taking care of the masters for whom the servant works. This servant is taking care of all sentient beings, pacifying their suffering and bringing them happiness. Since, for their happiness and success, the people who own a company or factory need people to work for them, taking care of the employees is like taking care of the owners. By thinking in this way, you put on clothes not just for your own sake but also for the sake of all sentient beings.

When you eat, again remember, "I'm responsible for bringing happiness to all sentient beings and pacifying all their suffering. This is the purpose of my life. Again, to do this I need to be healthy and have a long life, so I'm eating this food in order to be able to serve other sentient beings." Eating the food then becomes work for the happiness of all sentient beings.

When you then go to work, again remember your universal responsibility, and especially remember the people who employ you. If they didn't employ you, you wouldn't have your present comfort. If nobody employed you, you couldn't even survive as a human being. Your present enjoyments derive from the kindness of the people who have given you a job.

First remember your universal responsibility: "I'm responsible for all sentient beings, for bringing them happiness and for pacifying all their suffering." Then, remembering the kindness of the people who have employed you, think, "I'm going to serve all sentient beings, in particular my employers and the people who use these products. All those people and animals need this food (clothing or whatever the product is)." By doing your work, you help bring comfort to many human beings and even dogs, cats and other animals. Remember how your work benefits many sentient beings, bringing them comfort and enjoyment. This is logical—it doesn't require you to have any particular faith.

Remember, "I'm offering this service because they need me for their happiness and enjoyment." In this way you can go to work with much happiness and satisfaction. If you leave your home thinking only about your own happiness and problems, there's no enjoyment in your life. You then go to work with an unhappy mind and are unhappy while you work. Your mind is unhappy all day. If your mind is under the control of self-cherishing, it makes your life boring and exhausting.

When you go to bed, again remember, "I'm responsible for the happiness of all sentient beings. Since the purpose of my life is to serve them, I need to be healthy and have a long life. For that reason I'm going to sleep." You thus sleep for the benefit of all sentient beings.

If you live your life from morning until night with this attitude of universal responsibility, all your actions—eating, drinking, sitting, sleeping, working, talking and so forth—become virtue, pure virtue. Why is this so? Since your actions are unstained by self-cherishing, they become not only virtue but pure virtue. With this attitude everything you do from morning to night becomes the unmistaken cause of happiness. It results only in happiness. This happiness comes from your own mind. By transforming your mind into the cause of happiness, you create happiness, the happiness of this life and the lives after this, and even the peerless happiness of full enlightenment. Everything comes from your mind. You create everything from your own mind.

Making parties meaningful

When we give a party, we usually do it with attachment clinging to this life, to our own happiness and good reputation. That attitude is one of worldly concern, or worldly desire. When we give a party with that attitude, since our motivation is non-virtuous, all our actions become non-virtuous.

How do we transform the action of giving a party into something positive? How do we make it a true cause of happiness? Again, by remembering universal responsibility: "I'm responsible for pacifying the sufferings of all sentient beings and bringing them happiness. For that reason, I need to develop my mind in the path, especially in compassion and altruism. To develop my mind for the benefit of sentient beings, I need to create the necessary condition of merit, or good karma. Therefore, I'm going to make charity of this food and drink to my kind mother sentient beings, from whom I receive all my past, present, and future happiness." Giving a party in this way becomes Dharma.

With an attitude of universal responsibility, from morning to night our actions become Dharma. They are virtuous, or positive, the unmistaken causes of happiness. Since everything—happiness and suffering—comes from our own mind, we have great freedom to stop suffering and to find happiness.

Columbia University, New York
6 September 1990

··· 2 ···

How Things Exist

Motivation

ALL OUR HAPPINESS and suffering comes from our own mind. As our actions depend on our mind, we should first generate the motivation of bodhicitta, the highest, purest motivation. Our motivation for listening to [or reading] this teaching should be unstained by worldly concern seeking the happiness of only this life; it should also not be one of seeking the happiness of even future lives, which is still temporary samsaric happiness. Furthermore, we should not have a motivation seeking even ultimate happiness for self. What should our motivation be? It should be one of wishing to achieve full enlightenment for the sake of only other sentient beings, who equal the extent of infinite space. Think, "In order to free other sentient beings from all their sufferings and obscurations and lead them to full enlightenment, I am going to listen to this teaching on the graduated path to enlightenment." It is extremely important to listen to the teachings with this altruistic attitude.

Tonight I would like give those who'd like to receive them the oral transmission of the *Foundation of All Good Qualities*, a *lam-rim* prayer that is a meditation on the whole graduated path to enlightenment,[4] and the mantras of Avalokiteshvara, the Buddha of Compassion; Manjushri, the Buddha of Wisdom; Vajrapani, the Buddha of Power; and Shakyamuni Buddha, the kind, compassionate founder of the teachings that we study and practice.

The nature of the enlightened mind

Before giving the oral transmission of the prayer of the graduated path to enlightenment I should say something about its significance.

Enlightenment is the state of mind that has ceased all faults—all defilements, or obscurations—and perfected all qualities, or realizations, of the path. We can experience this state called "full enlightenment" or "buddhahood" on this mental continuum. By training our mind in the path to enlightenment, we can establish this state of peerless happiness and perfect peace on the continuation of our present consciousness; we do so through the skillful means of method and wisdom.

By generating the path contained in the lam-rim teachings, we can achieve any happiness we seek. We can gain the happiness of this life, the happiness of future lives and, more importantly, ultimate happiness, the cessation of all suffering and its causes. Even more importantly, however, we can achieve the state of mind that is completely pure, having ceased even the subtle obscurations, which interfere with our consciousness directly perceiving all past, present

[4] This prayer was composed by Lama Tsongkhapa. See Appendix 1, *The Joy of Compassion* or online at www.LamaYeshe.com.

and future existence. The obscurations to the fully knowing mind interfere with the continuation of our consciousness becoming omniscient mind. The state of omniscient mind has ceased all gross and subtle obscurations, even the subtle imprints left by the ignorance that apprehends true existence and produces the truly existent appearance, or dual view. When even these subtle obscurations are purified, or ceased, our consciousness is fully developed with respect to understanding, or realization, and becomes omniscient.

A small mirror can reflect an entire city or the thousands of objects in a supermarket. If that mirror doesn't have dirt or any other material obscuring it we can see everything very clearly in it. It is similar with our consciousness, which becomes omniscient when all our obscurations have been eradicated by our generating the remedy of the path. This omniscient state is known as "full enlightenment," "buddhahood" or "the non-abiding sorrowless state." And the ultimate nature of that omniscient mind is emptiness, or *shunyata*.

What's the purpose of achieving this state? It is so that we can perfectly guide sentient beings. Once we have achieved the omniscient mind, we can see the mind of every sentient being; we can see the characteristics, karma and level of mind of every sentient being and every single method that fits them. We can then guide them from happiness to happiness to full enlightenment, the perfect state of peace. With the omniscient mind that sees every single sentient being's characteristics and level of mind, as well as the various methods to guide them, we can free them from the different levels of sufferings and obscurations. We also have the perfect power to reveal those methods to them. By manifesting various forms—even hundreds or thousands of forms for a single sentient being—we can reveal the various methods to guide sentient beings along the path to happiness. In this way, we can gradually lead them to full enlightenment.

At that time we have also completed the training of our mind in compassion for every sentient being. Once we have achieved full enlightenment, it is mainly compassion that makes us work for every sentient being, bringing them from happiness to happiness to full enlightenment. We have great compassion for every sentient being without discrimination, without depending on whether that sentient being likes, makes offerings to or praises us. A buddha, a fully enlightened being, doesn't discriminate between somebody who cuts one side of his body with a knife and another person who puts perfume on the other side of his holy body. Even though one person is harming and the other helping, there is no discrimination from the side of the enlightened being. There's equal compassion for both the person who harms with a knife and the one who offers perfume. There's no discriminating thought. Buddha doesn't feel more compassion for someone who helps him and less or no compassion for someone else who cuts his body piece by piece. Buddha has no thought not to work for and help the sentient being who harms him. Buddha has exactly the same compassion for both sentient beings, and because of that, Buddha works for both sentient beings without discrimination.

Because the Buddha's great compassion for every sentient being is equal, each sentient being receives guidance according to the level of their mind. Buddha manifests in various forms. For those who have pure minds, Buddha manifests in pure forms; for those who have impure minds, Buddha manifests in impure, or ordinary, forms. Buddha manifests as whatever is necessary to guide a particular sentient being. Buddha can manifest as a king, minister, judge, monk, man, woman or even prostitute, butcher or hungry ghost. As sentient beings have various karmas and various characteristics of mind, one single method cannot suit everyone. We need to manifest in various forms to communicate with and guide sentient beings and have to reveal the various teachings according to their level of mind. After we become a fully enlightened being, we guide sentient beings by revealing various means with our body, speech and mind. We then effortlessly and perfectly guide all sentient beings without the slightest mistake.

When the sun rises, even though there's only one sun, it is reflected in every body of water on earth, from tiny drops of dew on plants to great oceans. As long as the water isn't covered, the sun is reflected in it. But the sun doesn't have a motivation to be reflected in the water; it doesn't have to put any effort into it—those reflections spontaneously appear. Similarly, after we achieve full enlightenment we spontaneously, perfectly guide sentient beings by revealing various means with our holy body, speech and mind.

Levels of happiness

The ultimate goal of meditating, of practicing Dharma, is to bring happiness to every sentient being—but not just the happiness of this life, which means physical and mental comfort, but more importantly long-term happiness, the happiness of all the coming future lives. In other words, our aim is to bring others happiness until they cut the continuation of the cycle of death and rebirth. Until we break the continuity of this suffering, we have to circle continuously, experiencing the suffering of rebirth and death again and again.

How long does it take to be completely free from the cycle of death and rebirth? It depends on whether or not we meet the right path, whether or not we understand that path, and whether or not we practice it. And even if we practice the right path, how quickly we achieve liberation from the suffering cycle of death and rebirth depends on how skillfully we practice it.

Our goal is to lead sentient beings to long-term happiness, the happiness of future lives. However, a much more important goal than that is to bring them to ultimate happiness, to the complete end of all suffering and its causes, karma and disturbing thoughts. This ultimate happiness means that they never experience at all the sufferings of rebirth, old age, sickness, death, or any other problem. To bring sentient beings this ultimate happiness of liberation is much more important than to bring them the happiness of future lives.

However, the most important thing of all is to bring sentient beings to the peerless happiness of full enlightenment. The happiness of this life and the happiness of future lives are still temporary, and even the ultimate happiness of liberation is just liberation for the self from true suffering and the true cause of suffering. Among all the kinds of happiness that we can bring other sentient beings, the most important is that of full enlightenment, the state that has ceased all faults of the mind and perfected all realizations. This state of full enlightenment is complete peace of mind. Until we achieve full enlightenment, we've neither gained complete peace of mind nor fully developed our mind's capacity to understand all existence.

We are responsible for pacifying the sufferings of all sentient beings and for obtaining their happiness and there are these different levels of happiness that we can bring them. The question is, "How can I benefit other sentient beings?" Sentient beings don't want to receive harm from you. Just like you, every other sentient being wants happiness and doesn't want suffering, not even the slightest discomfort in a dream. Since all they want is happiness, the benefit we should offer other sentient beings is to bring them what they want and not what they don't want, which is suffering. And while we should bring them the benefit of the comfort and happiness of this life, it's more important that we bring them the greater benefit of long-term happiness, the happiness of future lives. An even more important benefit that we should bring others is ultimate happiness, the complete end of all suffering and its causes. However, the greatest benefit that we should offer sentient beings, what they're missing and what they really need, is the peerless happiness of full enlightenment. This state of complete peace of mind is the greatest benefit we can bring sentient beings.

Even if sentient beings don't know what full enlightenment, or buddhahood, means, even if they don't talk about it or think about it, you can see from the way they live their everyday lives that this is what they are looking for. Even if they don't talk about it, this is what they need. For example, when people do business, according to the funds they have, according to what they can afford, they look for the business that makes the greatest profit. They look for the greatest profit from the money they spend. Actually, their wish is to have the greatest profit in the world. Even when they go shopping, they buy the best quality things, those that will last the longest. They buy the best quality food. According to their capacity, they try to get whatever is the best.

From examining their wishes in everyday life we can understand that even though they might not talk about the happiness of future lives, the ultimate happiness of liberation, or the highest happiness of full enlightenment, others always choose the things of best quality. It is only because of their ignorance that they don't know that these things, especially full enlightenment, are what they need to achieve.

Purifying the mind

We have the responsibility of bringing others to the peerless happiness of full enlightenment. Why are we responsible? Because we have received a perfect human rebirth. First of all, the nature of our mind is clear light. We have a mind that has buddha-nature, the nature of a fully enlightened being.

The sky is not oneness with clouds. Clouds are temporary; they come and go. Depending on causes and conditions, clouds come; depending on other causes and conditions, they go, and the sky becomes clear. It's the same with a mirror: depending on causes and conditions, it can be obscured by dirt; depending on other causes and conditions, the dirt obscuring the mirror can be cleaned away. The mirror was only temporarily obscured.

Our mind is like that. Its nature is clear light and the obscurations—ignorance, attachment, anger and the other disturbing thoughts—are temporary, not permanent. Due to causes and conditions, our mind is obscured, but due to other causes and conditions, the obscurations can be cleared away and we can be free from fear, guilt and all other undesirable emotions.

It all depends on how we live our life, on what we do with our mind. One way of acting obscures our mind; another way of acting frees it from obscurations and it then becomes fully awakened. It even depends on the actions we do each day: one action can obscure our mind; another can thin our obscurations and free our mind.

How we live our life, what we do with our body, speech and mind, has different effects on our mind. Different actions have different effects but it mainly depends on the kind of attitude we have when we act. When we act with a negative attitude, with ignorance, attachment, anger or another disturbing thought, it affects our mind; it obscures it. But when we live our life with non-ignorance, non-attachment, non-hatred and other positive attitudes, the effect is positive. It diminishes our obscurations; it purifies or lessens them.

When we practice Dharma, depending how skillfully we practice, it immediately purifies our mind. Our mind is purified that much; our obscurations become that much thinner. But when we act with body, speech and mind out of ignorance, attachment, anger and other negative attitudes, it further obscures our mind. It produces more confusion in our daily life and in the long-term, in our future lives. It's a dependent arising, like the examples of the clouds in the sky and the dirt on a mirror.

We experience various kinds of suffering and happiness because of the different negative and positive attitudes we generate in living our life. Because of those attitudes we experience suffering and happiness.

How the mind exists

The nature of our mind is clear light; it is empty of existing from its own side. The mind is a phenomenon that the self possesses.[5] It is non-substantial, colorless, shapeless and clear in nature; it has the ability to perceive objects; and it is not an object of the five senses. That is one way to define the mind. In dependence upon this base, a phenomenon that has such characteristics, we have labeled, or merely imputed, "mind." Therefore, there's no mind existing from its own side; there's no real mind from its own side. Mind is nothing other than that which we have merely imputed by our mind in dependence upon that base, that particular phenomenon. Therefore there's no such thing as a real mind from its own side. The mind is empty of existing from its own side. That is one definition of the clear light nature of the mind, which refers to its ultimate nature.

This ultimate nature of the mind, this clear light nature, is not oneness with the obscurations, the disturbing thoughts. Because of that, in dependence upon causes and conditions, obscurations can be eliminated.

[5] In the sense that we talk about "my mind."

There's no real mind from its own side; there's no unlabeled mind. The way the mind exists is being merely imputed by the mind in dependence upon that phenomenon with the particular character- istics mentioned above. Therefore, the mind is labeled; the way the mind exists is being imputed by the mind to that particular base. Mind exists in dependence upon that particular base, the particular phenomenon that is non-substantial, colorless, shapeless, clear in nature and able to perceive objects. Mind exists in dependence upon that base and upon the thought that labels it "mind." In other words, mind exists in mere name. What is called "mind" is a name, and a name has to come from the mind, has to be imputed by the mind. There is no mind existing from its own side. Mind comes from the mind.

The mind that exists is the labeled mind, not the unlabeled mind. The mind that appears to us as unlabeled is a hallucination. That mind doesn't exist. The mind that appears to be real from its own side doesn't exist. That independent, unlabeled mind is not true. It's false. No such thing exists in reality. In reality the mind is empty; it is empty of existing from its own side.

When a magician transforms a piece of wood or a stone into a beautiful man or woman, he uses the power of mantras or the power of substances to hallucinate the senses of the people in the audience. When the people who are watching see the beautiful man or woman and start to believe that what appears to them is true, their concept is wrong. Why is it a wrong concept? Because that beautiful man or woman that their mind apprehends, or believes in, doesn't exist. A beautiful man or woman appears to the audience, whose senses have been made defective by the power of mantras or substances, but it doesn't exist. It appears but it doesn't exist.

The magician and also anyone whose eye sense has not been made defective by the power of mantras or substances understand that the people who believe in that real man or woman are wrong. They can see that concept is wrong. Even the people themselves will later realize that their concept is false. When they discover for themselves that it was just a transformation performed by the magician, they will see that their previous concept was wrong. Why? Because the object they believed they saw doesn't exist.

It is the same with the mind and the I, or self. They are empty of existing from their own side.

How a table exists

To give a clearer idea of this, I often use the simpler example of a table. Even though this way of analyzing is not the correct way to meditate on emptiness, it gives you an idea of the correct way to meditate. Especially if you're a beginner, it will give you some idea of how the table exists in reality, of what the table is.

When a person first enters this hall, they see that there is a table here in front of me. But what makes the person decide to give the name "table" to this particular object and not to the steps or to the throne? What makes the person decide to give this object the label "table"? There has to be a reason before deciding on the label "table." The reason is that the person sees, first of all, a material object that performs the function of supporting things, or of allowing things to be put on top of it. The person first seeing that becomes the reason to label "table." That is what makes the person decide, among the numberless labels, on this particular label, "table."

Seeing this object that performs the function of supporting things is the reason in the mind of the person for applying the label "table." There has to be a reason before the label is applied, and the reason is seeing the basis for the label. You see the base first, then you apply the label, "It's a table." Therefore, this material object that you first see, which can perform the function of supporting things, is not table. This is the base. You see the base first, which is the reason to give the label "table."

Otherwise, if seeing the base doesn't come first, you haven't got any reason to label "table." There's no reason in your mind for you to label this "table," that "steps," or that "throne." There's no reason to make you decide to give a particular label.

If the first thing you see is the table, if you see the table before giving the label "table," there would be no reason to label "table." Since it's already table, why would you label "table" on the table? There would be no reason to do that.

For example, when parents name their child Jeff, they label on something that is not Jeff. Labeling "Jeff" on something that is not Jeff has meaning. But if the base, the aggregates, were already Jeff, there would be no purpose in labeling "Jeff" on Jeff. You would then again have to label "Jeff" on Jeff; then you would again have to label "Jeff" on Jeff…. It would become endless.

This is one logical reasoning used in the four-point analysis.[6] The first of the four points is recognizing the object to be refuted. The second point is that of ascertaining the pervasion, that if anything exists it should exist either one with its base or separately from its base. If the I is truly existent, it has to exist either one with the aggregates or separately from the aggregates.

If the I is one with the aggregates, various mistakes arise. The I is the receiver and the aggregates, this body and mind, are what is received. So, the receiver and what is received would then become one. In other words, the I, the possessor, and the aggregates, the possession, would become one. So, there is no way that the possessor and the possession can be one. They have to be different.

Anyway, if you see the table first, what reason do you have to label it "table"? There's no reason to label "table" on that which is already table. It has no meaning, no purpose. Normally, you see the base and then say, "I see the table." In order to see the table, you have to see the base of the table first. Otherwise, there's no reason for you to say, "I see the table." By seeing the base, this object that you can put things on top of, you then label "I see the table" and believe in that label.

By seeing the base of these steps, you say, "I see the steps," and by seeing the base of this throne, you say, "I see the throne." By seeing

[6] That is, if the I were one with the aggregates, labeling "I" would be superfluous. It would simply be one more name for the aggregates. The four points are (1) recognizing the object to be refuted, (2) ascertaining the pervasion of the two possibilities of oneness and difference, (3) ascertaining the lack of oneness of the I and the aggregates, and (4) ascertaining the lack of difference of the I and the aggregates.

a particular object and the particular function that it performs, you then label, "I see the table," "I see the steps" or "I see the throne."

Seeing the base has to come first. This thing that performs the function of supporting things is not the table. This thing that you climb up is not the steps. This thing that you sit on is not the throne. The thing that performs the function of supporting things is the base to be labeled "table." This is one point to meditate on to find out what the table is. Since you use this base as a reason to label "table," it's not the table, just as this is not the steps and this is not the throne.

Even from this analysis, you can see that the table and the base to be labeled "table," the steps and the base to be labeled "steps" and the throne and the base to be labeled "throne" are different. They don't exist in the way we normally think they do, which is that this concrete thing itself is the table and that is the steps and that is the throne.

Another point is that you talk about the parts of a table. When you say "the parts of the table," it means the parts of the table are not the table. This top is not the table, this leg is not the table, this leg is not the table, that leg is not the table, and that leg is not the table. Just from the language, you can tell that saying "the parts of the table" means they're not the table.

Even the whole group of all these parts gathered together is not the table. What is it? It is the base to be labeled "table." None of these parts is the table, and even the whole group of all the parts is not the table. This is clear.

Another point is that the table is nowhere on this. There's no table here or there or there. There's no table on this base.

The first point is that the base is not the table. When you come into the room, how do you come to apply labels to things? You can see that the reason you use to apply a label to something is not that thing. You use seeing the base of the table as the reason to label "table," but this object that can be used to put things on is not table. You apply the label "table" after seeing the base. It's clear that the base and the label are different.

The second point is that none of the parts of the table is the table. And even the whole group of all the parts is not the table. It is the base to be labeled "table." It now becomes clearer that the table is different from its base.

The third point is that you cannot find the table anywhere on this base. But that doesn't mean there's no table in this room; it doesn't mean the table doesn't exist. The table exists in this room—there are actually many tables here in this room. There's no table here on this, but there is a table in this room. This makes clear what the table is.

This is not the correct way to meditate on emptiness, since this way of searching for the table is related to the merely imputed table and leaves out the truly existent table. We haven't touched the object to be refuted, the truly existent table, which we are supposed to realize is empty. Therefore, according to Lama Tsongkhapa and many other great pundits, this is not the correct way of analyzing.

In this way of analyzing, when you search for the table among all its parts, you find that none of the parts is the table, and even the whole group of all the parts is not the table but the base to be labeled table. But it doesn't mean that the table doesn't exist. The table exists.

So, what is that table? Because we see this object that performs the function of allowing things to be put on top of it, we merely impute "table" and believe it is a table. Because this object is here in this room, we believe that there is a table in this room. By seeing this object, we believe, "I see a table." It is a concept. By seeing this object in this room, we merely impute, "There is a table." We leave it just at that; we are satisfied just by that. There's no table anywhere on this, but there is a table in this room.

You can see now that the way the table exists is *extremely* subtle. When you really analyze what the table is, it is *extremely* subtle. It is not that the table is nonexistent, but it is *like* it is nonexistent. It is not nonexistent because you can make the table, use the table, break the table. If you make this base, you believe, "I made a table"; you simply believe, "I made a table." If you use the table, you believe, "I'm using the table"; you simply believe, "I'm using the table." And if you break the table, you believe, "I broke the table."

The table is not nonexistent, but it is not the concrete thing that we normally think it is. We normally think of the table as something concrete that is oneness with its base, undifferentiable from its base. We can't split the base and the label "table." There is something concrete there. So, that is not table. There's no table on this, but there is a table in this room.

You can now see how the table is completely empty. It has no existence from its own side. There's no real, concrete table from its own side. From this you can get an idea of how the table exists. It is extremely subtle.

After this analysis, you know that none of the parts is the table and even the whole group of the parts is not the table. There's no table anywhere here on this base, but there is a table in this room. By analyzing like this, you see that the way the table exists is extremely fine, extremely subtle, but when you check what is appearing to you, you find that a real, concrete table is left there, oneness with its base. This is what is called *the object to be refuted.* That real table appearing from its own side, that truly existent table, that independent table, is the object to be refuted. That concrete thing left there is the object to be refuted, and it is a hallucination. In reality it is completely empty.

This is the correct way to meditate on the emptiness of the table. By recognizing that the table appears to you to be independent, unlabeled, real from its own side, you then search for that table to see whether or not it exists. When you don't find it and you see that it's empty, at that time you're seeing the emptiness, or ultimate nature, of the table. By seeing the ultimate truth of the table, that it is completely empty of existing from its own side, as a result you then realize the conventional truth of the table, that the table exists in mere name, being merely imputed by the mind. This is subtle dependent arising.

The fourth of the four schools of Buddhist philosophy, the Madhyamaka, has two divisions, Svatantrika and Prasangika. This is the Prasangika view of the subtle dependent arising of the table, the conventional truth of the table: the table exists in mere name, being merely imputed by the mind.

How Zopa exists

In the same way, this body is not Zopa and this mind is not Zopa. None of these five aggregates—form, feeling, recognition, compounding aggregates or consciousness—is Zopa. Even the whole group of these aggregates is not Zopa: it is the base to be labeled "Zopa." You can find Zopa nowhere on the group of all these aggregates, on the association of this body and this mind. But it doesn't mean there's no Zopa. Zopa exists in this hall. There's no other reason at all that there's Zopa in this hall, except that these aggregates, this body and mind, are here in this hall. This is the only reason that it is believed there is Zopa in this hall. Again, what Zopa is is extremely fine, extremely subtle.

How the I exists

It is the same with the I, which is the main one we should understand. Our body is not the I; nor is our mind—the association of body and mind is the base to be labeled "I." When we say "my body and mind" or "my aggregates," we can see that the I is the possessor and they are the possession. It's clear even from this that they're not the I. Our body is not the I; our mind is not the I. None of these aggregates is the I; even the whole group of the aggregates is not the I.

However, that doesn't mean that there's no I. The I is in this hall but there's no other reason to believe this except that the base, the aggregates, are now in this hall. If somebody asked, "Where are

you?" we'd reply, "I'm in the United States, in New York, in Columbia University, in the hall," but the only reason we'd have for saying
that would be that our aggregates are here in the United States, in
New York, in this Columbia University hall. Just because of that, we
believe, "I'm here in this hall."

The I that exists is nothing other than that which is merely imputed
by the mind in dependence upon the aggregates. That's all it is.

From birth, from morning to night, the I that appears to us and in
which we believe is completely contradictory to its reality. The I that
exists is completely other than that which appears to us and which
we apprehend. The I that exists is not the I that appears to us and in
which we believe. It is the same as with the table and all those other
examples. Their reality is something other than that which normally
appears to us and in which we normally believe.

The I is completely empty of existing from its own side. There's
no real I (in the sense of one existing from its own side), no independent I, no unlabeled I. When somebody criticizes us, we normally
think that they are really hurting this I, which is a real one existing
from its own side. We then get angry with that person and want to
harm them. When somebody praises us, we think that they are praising this real I, which is something real from its own side. We then
become excited and attached to that person. We want to help them,
but not the other person who has criticized us.

In reality, this real I is like something in a dream. It doesn't exist.
We are always concerned about this I and worried that somebody
might hurt it: "My friend might leave me" or "This person might hurt
me." However, the object that appears to us and in which we believe

doesn't exist. That real I, the I existing from its own side, is a complete hallucination. It's completely empty.

We have to think of the reality of how the I exists; we have to think of the subtle dependent arising or the emptiness of the I (which means the same thing). Thinking of the emptiness of the I brings the understanding that the I is a dependent arising; thinking that the I is a dependent arising, merely imputed by the mind in dependence upon the aggregates, allows us to see that the I is empty.

When we practice awareness that the I is a dependent arising or that the I is empty, when somebody criticizes us it's like somebody criticizing us in a dream. There's no subject to be harmed and there's no object, somebody giving harm. Even though such things appear, since they don't exist, there's no point in getting angry or in having the dissatisfied mind of desire. There's no point in having so much clinging or anger or ignorance. There's no point in having the concept of true existence, the false concept that believes that there's an independent I, an unlabeled I, a truly existent I.

What is the I? The I is a dependent arising; it exists in dependence upon its base—the aggregates—and the mind that labels it. Therefore, the I is empty of existing from its own side. This is the reality of the I.

By realizing this ultimate nature of the I, we eliminate the wrong conception that the I, which is imputed, has an existence from its own side, as it appears to have, and clinging to that as true. This thought is a wrong concept because the object in which it believes doesn't exist.

When the people in the audience discover that the beautiful man or woman who appeared to them and in whom they believed is a transformation by the magician, they then discover that their previous belief was wrong. Their concept of that beautiful man or woman as real is stopped.

Similarly, by realizing the ultimate nature of the I and by developing this wisdom, we eliminate the ignorance that believes in true existence. By eliminating this ignorance and the seed of this ignorance, we then eliminate all the other delusions that arise from it: attachment, anger and the rest of the six root delusions and the twenty secondary delusions as well.[7] All those disturbing thoughts and karma are terminated. Since the true cause of suffering has been eradicated, all true suffering ceases: the hell sufferings of heat and cold, the hungry ghost sufferings of hunger and thirst, the animal sufferings of being foolish and being eaten by other animals, the human sufferings of rebirth, old age, sickness and death, and all the *deva* sufferings. The devas who are worldly gods experience the sufferings of the signs of death and so forth and the gods in the form and formless realms experience pervasive compounding suffering, the suffering of being under the control of delusion and karma. All these sufferings cease.

Since there's no cause of suffering left within our consciousness, no ignorance or even a seed of it, it's impossible for suffering to arise again. In this way we achieve the ultimate happiness of liberation.

With this wisdom, we then practice bodhicitta, the skillful method of the Great Vehicle. By practicing method and wisdom together, we engage in the conduct of the six paramitas and then achieve

---

[7] For a description of the six root and twenty secondary delusions, see *Meditation on Emptiness*, pp. 255–66.

enlightenment. We can do this more quickly by practicing the skillful means of tantra. By developing wisdom and practicing the skillful means of tantra, we can achieve enlightenment in one lifetime, and by practicing together the special wisdom and greatest skillful means of Highest Yoga Tantra, method and wisdom unified, we can achieve enlightenment in not only one life but in the brief lifetime of this degenerate age,[8] in just a few years.

Oral transmissions

[Rinpoche gives the oral transmission of the lam-rim prayer, *Foundation of All Good Qualities*, in Tibetan.]

Receiving the transmission of this lam-rim prayer leaves on your consciousness an imprint to develop the entire graduated path to enlightenment. However, to receive realizations and thus fully develop the path within your mind, you need to rely upon the blessings, help and guidance of special deities. This requires you to do these deities' meditation-recitation and for that you need to receive the transmission of their mantras.

First I will give you the mantra of Avalokiteshvara, the Buddha of Compassion, who helps you develop especially the realizations of loving kindness, compassion and bodhicitta.

[Rinpoche gives the oral transmission of OM MANI PADME HUM.]

Now, in order to develop wisdom, you need to recite the mantra of Manjushri, the embodiment of all the buddhas' wisdom.

---

[8] A degenerate age (Skt: *kaliyuga*) has five characteristics: short life spans, scarce means of subsistence, mental afflictions, strong wrong views and weak sentient beings.

[Rinpoche gives the oral transmission of OM AH RA PA TSA NA DHIH.]

Now, in order to pacify obstacles to the success of your practice and generally to pacify all obstacles to achieving success and happiness in this and future lives and to achieving the ultimate happiness of enlightenment, you need to recite the mantra of Vajrapani, who pacifies obstacles such as disease and spirit harm and purifies negative karma. Some people have even recovered from cancer by doing the meditation-recitation of Vajrapani. It is very powerful and very effective for healing. Vajrapani, the embodiment of all the buddhas' power, has various aspects; this is the mantra of Vajrapani-Hayagriva-Garuda.

[Rinpoche gives the oral transmission of OM VAJRAPANI HAYAGRIVA GARUDA HUM PHAT.]

Reciting the mantra of the kind, compassionate Shakyamuni Buddha just once purifies 84,000 eons of negative karma. Please repeat this prayer and mantra.

[Rinpoche then gives the oral transmission of *Lama tön-pa chom-den-dä* [9] ... and TADYATHA OM MUNÉ MUNÉ MAHAMUNAYE SVAHA.]

Please dedicate by thinking, "I must free all sentient beings from all their suffering and its causes and lead them to full enlightenment. To do that, I'm going to achieve enlightenment. I therefore dedicate all my merits to achieve enlightenment for the sake of all sentient beings."

[9] See *Essential Buddhist Prayers*, Volume I, p. 26.

Thank you very much. I didn't get to explain the parts related to AIDS and the different thought transformation practices.[10] Anyway, there are many books on thought transformation, such as *Transforming Problems into Happiness* and *Seven-Point Thought Transformation*.[11] Anybody who wants to practice thought transformation should read those books and apply the teachings they contain to transform problems into happiness and achieve enlightenment for the benefit of all sentient beings, freeing them from all suffering, bringing them happiness and leading them to enlightenment.

The conclusion is, as I mentioned, that everything comes from the mind. The I, the table and so forth—everything comes from our own mind. Even our problems come from our own mind. You can also understand that the root of the whole of samsara, of all problems, is the concept of true existence. The concept of a truly existent I, of an I having existence from its own side, is the very root of all problems, of all suffering. In order to escape from suffering, we need to eliminate this root, and for that reason we need to understand the emptiness, or ultimate nature, of the I. That is the essence of this talk.

Thank you very much. I will pray for everybody. Thank you.

Columbia University, New York

7 September 1990

[10] The talks at Columbia University were originally advertised as "Transforming Problems."

[11] See the bibliography, p. 118. There are many English-language *Seven-Point* commentaries available, such as *Advice from a Spiritual Friend. The Kindness of Others* has an extensive list of them in its bibliography.

···3···

Lam-rim and Meditation on Emptiness

THE ESSENCE OF the teaching of the Buddha is the four noble truths, which are contained in this one verse:

Do not commit any non-virtuous actions,
Perform only perfect virtuous actions,
Subdue your mind thoroughly—
This is the teaching of the Buddha.[12]

Meditation on impermanence

The essence of what the next verse[13] says is to remember how the self, action, object, friend, enemy, stranger, our body and our possessions

[12] This verse comes in *Praise to Shakyamuni Buddha*, a prayer often recited before Buddhist teachings. See *Essential Buddhist Prayers*, Volume I, pp. 73–76.
[13] This verse, from *The Vajra Cutter Sutra*, also comes in *Praise to Shakyamuni Buddha*. Rather than reciting the actual verse, Rinpoche often uses it as the basis for meditation on impermanence and emptiness. However, it goes: "A star, a visual aberration, a flame of a lamp; an illusion, a drop of dew, or a bubble; a dream, a flash of lightning, a cloud—see conditioned things as such!" See http://www. fpmt.org/teachers/zopa/advice/vajracuttersutra.asp.

are transitory in nature. They change within every second by causes and conditions, and because of that, they can stop at any time. Therefore, it's not worthwhile to get angry, have the dissatisfied mind of desire or give rise to wrong conceptions, such as the concept of permanence. Believing these things, which are transitory in nature, to be something other than what they really are is the fundamental problem of life, the fundamental suffering in our life.

Being mindful of the nature of the self, action, object and these other things brings tranquility into our mind. It protects our mind; it protects us from disturbing thoughts, wrong conceptions. It protects us from all harmful thoughts and actions, or karma, which harm us and other sentient beings.

When we live our life with the concept of permanence and other mistaken thoughts, we look at things in a way that is contradictory to reality, a way in which they don't exist. Living like this brings confusion and thousands of problems into our life; it's living in a state of confusion.

Meditation on impermanence in everyday life—in other words, awareness of the reality of these things—is essential. It is the basis for happiness and peace of mind and the best protection for our life.

Meditation on emptiness

In addition to meditating on impermanence, we also have to meditate on emptiness.

Now, when we say, "I'm listening to Dharma," we're labeling what "I'm doing" in dependence upon what our aggregates, the association of our body and mind, are doing. By thinking of our aggregates and what they're doing, we label, "I'm listening to Dharma." If our aggregates are sitting on a chair, we say, "I'm sitting on a chair." When we think of the I, hear the word "I" or talk about the I, we're putting the label "I" on our aggregates.

When the I is doing the action of listening to teachings, since our mind is paying attention to the words, we impute, "I'm listening to teachings." And it's the same with the object, the teachings. The label "teachings" is imputed to the words that we hear, which were taught by Buddha.

When we think of our enemy or say or hear the word "enemy," again it is imputed; we've labeled some being "enemy." When we think of our friend, we apply the label "friend." We also apply the label "stranger" to the aggregates of someone we don't know.

When we see our possessions, again we apply the label "possessions" in dependence upon that particular base. It's the same with our body: when we think of our body or hear the word "body," again it's a label that we've imputed to the base of a torso with limbs and a head. In dependence upon that base we label "body."

From morning to night, no matter what we think, talk or hear about, we're thinking, talking or hearing about labels. We're labeling things every time we think. Every time we have a conversation at work or at home, we're constantly applying labels. We're making things exist by applying labels. Whenever we're thinking of anything, we're thinking about the labels, which are imputed.

Take, for example, the object that we label "clock." Each part of the clock has a label. Each label is applied to another label, which is applied to another label, which is applied to another label and so on down to the atoms—and even "atom" is a label that is merely imputed to another label. Atoms have particles, as was mentioned in the Prasangika Madhyamaka, one of the four Buddhist schools of philosophy, and discovered more recently by modern science.

One label is placed upon another label, which is placed upon another label and so on down to the atoms and their constituent particles. Since a clock is just a pile of labels, why do we see it as so concrete?

Everything—samsara and nirvana, suffering and happiness, the things we talk about from morning to night—is labeled. Everything comes from the mind, is imputed by the mind.

We can understand that a clock exists in dependence upon the particular base that performs the function of giving the time and the thought that labels it "clock." A clock is not independent; it doesn't exist from its own side. A clock is a dependent arising. It exists in dependence upon a base that performs the particular function of giving the time and the mind. Thus a clock is completely empty of existing from its own side.

A clock does not exist from there, from the side of the clock, but from the side of the mind. In the view of the mind, the perceiver, there's a clock. When we hear "clock," it means a dependent arising. A clock exists in dependence upon those two things—the appropriate base and the mind that labels it "clock." When we hear "clock," it means something that is merely imputed to a base by the mind. Clock itself is a dependent arising, a label, something imputed by the mind.

It is the same with the I. Again, "I" means a dependent arising. The I exists in dependence upon the aggregates and the thought that labels them "I." When you hear "I," it means a dependent arising, something labeled, or merely imputed, by the mind. Since "I" is a label, it comes from the mind. Thus the I is empty of existing from its own side.

It's the same with all the different sense objects: forms, sounds, smells, tastes and tangible objects. Again, they are nothing other than that which is merely imputed in dependence upon their base. That which is called "form" is what is labeled in dependence upon a base that has color and shape and is an object of the eye-sense. In dependence upon that particular base, "form" is merely imputed. Similarly with sound: "sound" is merely imputed by the mind to that particular phenomenon that the ear-sense is able to distinguish.

Forms, sounds, smells, tastes, tangible objects—they're all merely imputed by the mind in dependence upon becoming objects of particular senses. There's no such thing as real forms, real sounds, real smells, real tastes or real tangible objects from their own side. They are completely empty. What exists is only that which is merely imputed by the mind, that which comes from the mind. These phenomena exist but those other *real* phenomena do not. The forms, sounds, smells, tastes and tangible objects that appear to us as having nothing to do with our mind, as real from their own side, are complete illusions, or hallucinations.

All of samsara and nirvana, everything that we blab about from morning to night, exists in this way. All these things are empty of existing from their own side. What exists is what came from our mind, what is merely imputed by our mind.[14]

Practicing the good heart

It is extremely important to practice bodhicitta, or altruism, to obtain happiness for yourself and especially to obtain all happiness for all sentient beings.

In order to generate the realization of bodhicitta, the door to the Mahayana path to enlightenment, we need to generate the preliminary realization of renunciation of the whole of samsara. To generate renunciation of the whole of samsara we first need to generate renunciation of this life, to cut off clinging to this life. Worldly desire, which clings to this life, is the main obstacle to the actions of our body, speech and mind becoming Dharma. We have to cut off this worldly concern, which clings not only to our own happiness but also to just the happiness of this life; we have to free ourselves from this worldly concern, which is the basis of all the problems we experience in everyday life. This attachment is the main obstacle to Dharma practice and the basis of all confusion. In order to overcome this obstacle we need to meditate on the graduated path of the being of lower capability.

If there's no compassion within our mind, what we have is self-cherishing. Anger, the dissatisfied mind of desire, jealousy and all

---

[14] Because of recording problems, forty-five minutes of the teaching were missed at this point. Hence the sudden change of topic. (A few minutes were also missed at the very beginning of this talk.)

the other disturbing thoughts then arise because of that. The self-cherishing thought also interferes with our development of wisdom, our elimination of ignorance. In dependence upon self-cherishing we also follow ignorance.

Without the good heart, compassion, those other thoughts harm us and other sentient beings. From birth until now, when we haven't practiced loving kindness and compassion, when our mind has been under the control of self-cherishing and those other disturbing thoughts, we've given a lot of harm to other sentient beings. When our mind has not been patient or compassionate in nature, we've given harm to many other sentient beings even in this life, starting with the people and animals around us.

If we had completely eliminated these disturbing thoughts in the past, there'd be no reason for them to arise in this life, no reason to have been born with them. It's because we didn't eliminate them in our past lives that we've been born with this egocentric mind, self-cherishing thought and the other disturbing thoughts. Through beginningless rebirths we haven't eliminated self-cherishing, ignorance, anger, attachment or any other disturbing thought and with these thoughts we've been giving harm not only to ourselves but also to all the numberless other sentient beings. If we don't do something to change our attitude in this life, while we have this perfect human rebirth, if we don't do something to eliminate these disturbing thoughts, the same thing will also happen in our future lives. From life to life, continuously, we will give harm to other sentient beings as well as ourselves.

If we have the good heart, compassion for other sentient beings, all other sentient beings don't receive harm from us, starting with our family, the people closest to us, the ones we live, eat, work and deal with in everyday life. If we have the good heart, starting with our family and extending to include all other sentient beings, no one receives harm from us and everyone receives happiness. Not receiving harm from us is peace they receive from us. This peace is dependent upon us.

In addition, by having compassion within our mind, besides not giving harm to others, we benefit them, starting with the sentient beings closest to us and extending to all sentient beings. We benefit others, freeing them from suffering and bringing them happiness. This is the product of having compassion: we benefit others with our actions.

If we have the good heart, all others receive peace and happiness; if we don't have the good heart, if we don't change our attitude but allow our mind to be under the control of self-cherishing and the other disturbing thoughts, everyone receives harm from us, starting with the sentient beings closest to us and extending to all sentient beings. Therefore, we are completely responsible for the happiness of all sentient beings. Each of us is completely responsible for pacifying the sufferings of all sentient beings and bringing all of them temporary and, especially, ultimate happiness.

It doesn't matter whether or not the rest of our family practices compassion. It doesn't matter even if they hate us and only harm us. It doesn't matter even if the many millions of people in our country hate us and only harm us. Even if every sentient being hates and only harms us, there's nothing much to be depressed about because we're just one person. Even if we are suffering, even if we are born in hell, since we're just one person, there's nothing much to be depressed about. Even if we achieve liberation, ultimate happiness for ourselves, there's nothing much to be excited about because we are just one person, just one living being.

However, if we, the one person, don't have any compassion in our heart, there's a danger that we will harm numberless other sentient beings. This is much more terrifying. It has happened many times in the world that one person has killed many millions of people. By not practicing patience, by not practicing the good heart, one person can give great harm to millions of people, not to mention the animals in ocean and on the ground that are also harmed or killed.

If we ourselves don't practice the good heart there's the danger of our harming numberless other sentient beings. For us, the one person, to first practice the good heart is crucial. It's so important for other sentient beings. It's important for the person we live with and even more important if there are five or ten other people in our family. For the millions of people in your country it becomes even more important that we practice the good heart. And it is even more important for the numberless human beings, hell beings, hungry ghosts, animals, asuras and suras. Since suffering sentient beings are numberless, the need for every single person to practice the good heart becomes of the utmost importance.

We must practice the good heart. We must generate altruism toward other sentient beings. In our actions we must abandon giving harm to others and in addition we must benefit them. Even if we can't benefit others at least we shouldn't harm them. The very minimum practice is not to harm other sentient beings. If we can't stop giving harm to other sentient beings, there's no spiritual practice, no Dharma practice, left.

Levels of benefit

On the basis of not giving harm to others, we then benefit them. Benefiting other sentient beings doesn't mean causing them only temporary physical and mental happiness in this life. It is more important to cause others to have long-term happiness, happiness in all their future lives. Bringing them this benefit is more important because it's for such an incredible length of time—until they stop the suffering cycle of death and rebirth by generating the remedy of the path in their mind. Until then, they have to be reborn and die, continuously experiencing suffering. We need to bring others this long-term benefit, happiness in all their future lives, which is more important than bringing them temporary comfort and happiness in this life.

More important than simply bringing them happiness in all their future lives is completely ending all their suffering and its causes— delusion and karma—and bringing them ultimate happiness. This ultimate benefit is more important than the previous one, which involves bringing them temporary samsaric pleasure. No matter how much temporary pleasure we bring others, there's no end. They will continuously create samsara as long as they don't remove its causes—delusion and karma—including the ignorance not knowing the ultimate nature of the I, the aggregates, the mind and other phenomena. Until they eliminate their disturbing thoughts they will continue to produce karma and continuously create samsara by leaving imprints on their mental continua for the future-life samsara, the aggregates, which is the basis of rebirth, old age, sickness, death and all the many other human problems. Until they generate the path in their mind and eliminate the true cause of suffering, they will have to experience true suffering again and again. Since from their side they continuously create the cause of problems, their problems never end.

If we analyze even the temporary happiness that we bring others, we see that it is only suffering. Temporary samsaric pleasure is labeled "pleasure" and appears to be pleasure, but it is not pleasure. We label "pleasure" on a feeling that is suffering and it then appears to be pleasure. It's not real happiness, pure happiness. If it were pure happiness, the more we worked for it, the more it would increase day by day, month by month, year by year. But this isn't what happens—the more we work for it, the more the pleasure decreases and the discomfort increases.

Therefore, bringing others the ultimate benefit of cessation of all suffering and its causes is much more important than bringing them the happiness of future lives.

Now, the most important thing, even more important than this, is to bring all sentient beings to the perfect state of peace of full enlightenment. Full enlightenment, or buddhahood, is the mental state where all faults have ceased and all realizations have been completed. Bringing all sentient beings the ultimate benefit of full enlightenment is the most important thing of all.

In order to complete this work of bringing all sentient beings to full enlightenment, first we ourselves need to achieve full enlightenment. For that, we need to practice the lam-rim, the graduated path to enlightenment.

The three beings

The lam-rim has the graduated paths of the beings of three capabilities. The motivation of someone who practices the graduated path of the being of lower capability is that of having completely left this life behind, of having completely cut off clinging to this life. That attitude is generated by meditating on perfect human rebirth (how it is highly meaningful and will be difficult to achieve again), impermanence and death (death will definitely happen, it can happen at any moment, and at the time of death nothing—not our relatives, the people around us, our possessions nor our body—can benefit us except Dharma), and suffering. If we die without having purified our negative karma, by having created negative karma, after our death we will again take rebirth in one of the lower realms, in the hell, hungry ghost, or animal realm. If we were to be born there, we would have no happiness and no opportunity to practice Dharma. We would experience only the heaviest suffering. So, we also meditate on karma.

By generating the realizations of these meditations, we cut off clinging to this life. The aim of beings of lower capability is to achieve happiness in future lives, as a deva or human being, and in order to achieve this aim, they practice taking refuge and protecting karma. The main thing is protecting karma. We realize the shortcomings of the ten non-virtuous actions[15]—how harmful they are and how they are the cause of suffering—and see the benefits of living in vows of morality, such as abandoning the ten non-virtues, which means practicing the ten virtues. In other words, we protect karma and practice morality to achieve the happiness of future lives.

Beings of middling capability, on the basis of the motivation to cut off clinging to this life, then cut off clinging to the whole of samsara, to all samsaric perfections, or happiness. They don't have the slightest interest in samsara or in samsaric happiness and generate renunciation of the whole of samsara by meditating on the shortcomings of samsara: the general sufferings of samsara and the particular sufferings of the deva and human realms.

Their aim is to achieve liberation for self, release from samsara or, in other words, from true suffering and true cause of suffering. In order to achieve liberation for self, we practice the higher trainings of morality and concentration, which means *shamatha*, or tranquil abiding, and then on the basis of them, the higher training of great insight. The practice of the being of middling capability is also based on practice of the ten virtues, the practice of the being of lower capability. The difference is the goal.

Beings of great capability, with full renunciation of their own samsara, seeing it like being in the center of a fire, then look at how others are suffering in samsara and generate great compassion, feel-

---

[15] Of the ten non-virtuous actions, there are three of body (killing, stealing, sexual misconduct), four of speech (lying, speaking harshly, slandering, gossiping), and three of mind (covetousness, ill will, wrong views).

ing it unbearable that other sentient beings are experiencing the sufferings of samsara. Seeing other sentient beings suffering in samsara is like seeing them trapped in the center of a fire. There's no happiness at all, not even for a second. They feel unbearable compassion when they see how others are suffering.

The compassion that sees how others are suffering in samsara becomes a reason to generate the altruistic wish to free sentient beings from all their suffering and its causes. To be able to do that, we must be able to see all the different levels of mind of sentient beings. Take doctors, for example. Doctors cannot cure patients perfectly if they don't know all the sicknesses that they have and all the different treatments that should be given at different times, or even at the same time, to overcome their diseases. Doctors have to know every single diagnosis and every single treatment to be able to completely cure each patient. If doctors don't have that knowledge, they can't treat their patients perfectly. Similarly, we need to understand all the different levels of mind and characteristics of every sentient being and all the different methods needed to guide them, to free them from all their sufferings and obscurations and lead them to the peerless happiness of full enlightenment. Since only the omniscient mind can see all these things, we must achieve omniscient mind for the sake of all sentient beings, to free them from all their sufferings and lead them to enlightenment.

Compassion becomes the reason to generate bodhicitta, the altruistic wish to achieve enlightenment for all sentient beings. This is the motivation of beings of great capability. The aim of beings of great capability is to achieve enlightenment, or great liberation, for sentient beings. In order to achieve this aim, they practice the method of the bodhisattva's conduct, the six paramitas, and on top of that, those who practice tantra also practice the tantric path. In this way, they practice method and wisdom together.

Practice of the six paramitas and tantra by the being of great capability is based on both the practice of the three higher trainings of the being of middling capability and the practices of the being of lower capability, protecting karma and living in the morality of the ten virtues.

Other than these three types of beings, there are those who live just to obtain the happiness of this life. They're ordinary beings, not beings of real capability. Ordinary beings are those who don't attempt to obtain happiness beyond this life but just work for the happiness of this life alone. Their aim is nothing special, nothing higher than that of animals. Pigs, goats, cows, tigers, mice and even ants and other tiny insects are smart in finding themselves food and comfort and in destroying the enemies who harm them.

Such beings working just for the comfort of this life are ordinary beings. That is not the real meaning of human life. Even animals, non-human beings, can do this. The real meaning, the greatest meaning, of human life is, with bodhicitta, practicing the path of the six paramitas in order to achieve enlightenment for sentient beings. Lower than that is achieving liberation for self. Lower than that is achieving at least the happiness of future lives, long-term happiness beyond this life.

If we listen to Dharma teachings to achieve enlightenment for all sentient beings, it becomes a cause to achieve enlightenment for all sentient beings. If we listen to Dharma just to achieve liberation for ourselves, it becomes a cause of just that; it doesn't become a cause to achieve enlightenment. If we listen to Dharma to achieve the happiness of future lives, it becomes a cause of just that. It doesn't become a cause of enlightenment or of liberation for the self.

Now, if we listen to Dharma just for the happiness of this life, to get worldly power or a good reputation, even though the subject we listen to is Dharma, Buddha's teaching, our action of listening to Dharma does not become Dharma. Even though the subject is Dharma, the action of listening to the teaching doesn't become Dharma because the motivation isn't Dharma. It's a non-virtuous motivation of worldly concern, attachment clinging to this life.

Besides listening to Dharma, any action done with worldly concern, to obtain only the happiness of this life, becomes non-virtue. The result of non-virtuous actions is, as Lama Atisha explained, rebirth in the hell, hungry ghost or animal realm.

We can see that happiness and suffering come from our mind, not from outside. They come from our positive or negative attitudes in everyday life. It depends on how we think, on how we live our life every day. First of all, our happiness and suffering are not things that don't have a cause. There's no external creator who creates them. Our happiness and suffering are the creation of only our own mind in dependence upon our positive and negative attitudes.

Nagarjuna said that actions born from ignorance, anger and attachment are non-virtues and that all the suffering migratory beings arise from them. This means that all hell beings, hungry ghosts and animals arise from these non-virtues. Actions born from, or motivated by, the minds of non-ignorance, non-hatred and non-attachment are virtuous actions. From these virtuous actions, all the happy migratory beings arise.

From morning to night, twenty-four hours a day, everything depends on our attitude. When we have a positive attitude it produces the result of happiness; when we have a negative attitude it produces the result of suffering. The happiness we experience each day comes from our positive attitudes and the suffering we experience comes from our negative attitudes. Therefore, as we are the creator, we have great freedom. Since it's just up to our mind, we have great freedom to stop experiencing suffering and to obtain happiness by abandoning non-virtue and transforming our mind into virtue.

How Chiu-Nan exists

The creator of samsara, of all suffering and its causes, karma and all the other disturbing thoughts, is ignorance, the concept of true existence. This is the very root of the whole of samsara, of all problems, of true suffering and its causes, karma and all the rest of the disturbing thoughts, such as ignorance not knowing Dharma, attachment and anger. The very root is ignorance not knowing the ultimate nature of the I, or self. The very root is the concept of a truly existent self. To recognize this precisely, without mistake, is most important. Otherwise, there's no way that we can escape from the entire suffering of samsara. Unless we recognize the root, there's no way we can sever it.

Take Chiu-Nan,[16] for example. When there are these aggregates, this particular association of body and mind, but no thought to label them "Chiu-Nan," Chiu-Nan doesn't exist. Even though the aggregates are there, when there's no thought to label them "Chiu-Nan," Chiu-Nan doesn't exist at that time. And even if there were the thought in her parents' minds to label "Chiu-Nan," if there were no aggregates to label, again at that time Chiu-Nan wouldn't exist.

First we have to understand this clearly. When there are aggregates but no thought to label them "Chiu-Nan," Chiu-Nan doesn't exist. When there's a thought to label "Chiu-Nan" but no aggregates, also at that time Chiu-Nan doesn't exist.

Chiu-Nan comes into existence *only* when the base, the aggregates, are there and there is also a thought that labels them "Chiu-Nan." Only at that time does Chiu-Nan exist. So, Chiu-Nan exists in dependence upon the base, the association of body and mind, and the mind of the parents (or someone else) who label it "Chiu-Nan." In dependence upon these two—the base and the mind that labels "Chiu-Nan"—Chiu-Nan exists.

You can see that Chiu-Nan is merely imputed by the mind. Chiu-Nan exists being merely imputed by the mind in dependence upon those aggregates. Chiu-Nan is empty of existing from her own side. That is the reality of Chiu-Nan.

When we look at or think of Chiu-Nan, it is in dependence upon those particular aggregates that we label "Chiu-Nan." We don't see

---

[16] Chiu-Nan Lai arranged the talks at the Great Enlightenment Temple.

Chiu-Nan first. First we see that particular base, those particular aggregates, and seeing that makes us decide upon the particular label "Chiu-Nan." So, we don't see Chiu-Nan first. We see the base first and then we label it "Chiu-Nan." It is only after we label "Chiu-Nan" that Chiu-Nan then appears to us. Before we label "Chiu-Nan" there's no appearance of Chiu-Nan to us. The appearance of Chiu-Nan comes only after we have labeled the base.

But when Chiu-Nan appears to us she doesn't appear to be merely imputed by our mind. When we look at Chiu-Nan or think of her, we are not aware, or we forget, that Chiu-Nan is merely imputed. After we have labeled "Chiu-Nan," when Chiu-Nan then appears to us, she doesn't appear to be merely imputed. Chiu-Nan appears to be something real, something more than what is merely imputed. There is something extra, an unlabeled Chiu-Nan, which is completely opposite to the reality. The labeled Chiu-Nan is the reality but when she appears to us she doesn't appear that way.

We see an unlabeled, independent Chiu-Nan. We see Chiu-Nan, but in the aspect of not being merely labeled. Chiu-Nan is merely imputed, but on top of that merely labeled Chiu-Nan there's something extra, like a cloth covering a table. The merely imputed Chiu-Nan doesn't appear to us. The Chiu-Nan that appears to us is something else, something unlabeled, independent.

How Chiu-Nan appears to us is completely contradictory to the reality of how Chiu-Nan exists, as being merely imputed by our mind. This appearance of an unlabeled Chiu-Nan, a real Chiu-Nan, a Chiu-Nan from its own side, is false. Because it's contradictory to reality, it's false. If it accorded with reality, it wouldn't be false; but because it's opposite to the reality of how Chiu-Nan exists, it's false. So, this is the object to be refuted.

Seeing a snake at dusk

Imagine that at dusk you see a coiled multi-colored rope on a road. Because of the way the rope is coiled and because it's dusk and you can't see clearly, when you first see this form you label it "snake." After you label it "snake," a snake then appears to you. You're not aware, or you forget, that the snake that appears to you is merely imputed by your own mind. You are not aware of that because the snake doesn't appear to you as merely imputed.

First you see a coiled unclear form in the dusk. Before you apply the label "snake," there's no appearance of a snake to you. Only after you label "snake" and believe in your own label is there an appearance of a snake. The snake doesn't appear to be merely imputed. It appears to be a real snake, an unlabeled, independent snake. It appears to have existence from its own side.

This example is very easy to understand. There's no real snake there; there's no unlabeled, independent snake. Here in this case, there's not even a snake. You cannot find a snake on any of the parts of the rope or even on the whole group of the parts of the rope. You cannot find a snake anywhere there. You label "snake" and it then appears to you as a snake, but that snake doesn't even appear to be merely imputed; it appears to be unlabeled. The snake appears to you, the perceiver, to be an unlabeled, independent snake, until you shine a flashlight on it and see very clearly that it is a rope. Until that time, an unlabeled, independent snake appears to your senses, to your mind. You can see that this is completely false.

How the I exists

We can now relate this example to the I. We label "I" in dependence upon our aggregates. After the labeling of "I" is done, we believe in that label and I then appears to us. The thought that labels "I" is not the ignorance that is the root of samsara. That thought is not wrong.

First of all, it is clear that when we talk about "my body" or "my mind," I is the possessor and the body or mind is the possession. The possessor and the possession cannot be one; they are different. Therefore, my mind is not the I—the mind is the possession and I is the possessor. Since the I is the receiver and these aggregates are what are received, they are not one; they are different.

None of the five aggregates is the I. The aggregate of form is not the I, feeling is not the I, recognition is not the I, compounding aggregates are not the I, consciousness is not the I. Even the whole group of the five aggregates is not the I. The I cannot be found anywhere on these aggregates, from the top of the head down to the toes. The I exists nowhere, from the top of the head down to the toes. It is neither inside nor outside the body. The I exists nowhere on this body and mind. We cannot find it anywhere.

But there is an I in this temple. I am in this temple for no other reason than my aggregates, the association of my body and mind, are now here in this temple. Just because of this I believe, "I am now here in this temple." It is a concept, an idea. Because my aggregates are here, I believe, "I am here in this temple," but these aggregates are not the I, because they are the base to be labeled "I" and the I cannot be found anywhere on them. There's no I anywhere on these aggregates. First make that clear.

So, what is the I? How does the I exist? It becomes extremely fine, extremely subtle. There's no I on these aggregates, but there is I in this temple. What the I is is nothing other than what is merely imputed by the mind. That is the reality. That is what is called *subtle dependent arising* in the Prasangika view, which is very difficult to realize. How the I exists is extremely subtle. How the I exists is so subtle that it's easy to think that the I doesn't exist at all and fall into nihilism. It can be very dangerous. The Prasangika view of dependent arising is very subtle. It is not that the I doesn't exist but it's *as if* it doesn't exist. It's extremely fine, extremely subtle.

That is the reality of the I, but the I doesn't appear to us that way. It appears as something else: something concrete, unlabeled, independent, real. After the I is imputed, why does it appear truly existent? Why doesn't it appear merely imputed? Why doesn't it appear to us in accord with reality? Why does it appear as the opposite—unlabeled and existing from its own side?

The root of samsara

The thought that labels "I" in dependence upon the aggregates is not the ignorance that is the root of samsara. When the I appears to us, it appears to have existence from its own side, the complete opposite to being merely labeled. The later continuation of the thought that labels "I" starts to believe that the I, which is labeled, has existence from its own side, or true existence. The mind to which the truly existent I appears is still not the root of samsara. The root of samsara is the thought that believes, "This truly existent I that appears to me is true." Whenever we start to believe that the truly existent I is true, this is the concept of true existence and *this* is the root of samsara. This thought that believes the I is not merely labeled but has an existence from its own side is the root of samsara. Just that thought that believes this to be true is the root of samsara.

The wrong conceptions that believe the I to be permanent or to exist alone or with its own freedom without depending on the continuation of the aggregates are not the root of samsara. The root of samsara is just this thought. After the label "I" has been given, when the continuation of this thought starts to believe that the I has an existence from its own side, this is the root of samsara.

What makes the I, which is merely imputed, appear truly existent? Our past ignorance left an imprint on our mental continuum and this imprint is projected, like a projector projecting a film onto a screen or a TV channel showing people fighting, dancing, or doing other things. The imprint left on our mental continuum by past ignorance projects, or decorates, true existence onto the merely imputed I. We see a concrete I, and that is what the imprint left by ignorance has projected onto the mere I. That part is a complete hallucination.

Remember, as I told you before, how the clock is labeled on another label, which is labeled on another label. That is the reality, but for us there's a concrete clock from its own side. That hallucination of a concrete clock, a clock from its own side, is actually projected by the imprint left by past ignorance. This real I is projected by this ignorance in the same way. This real body and mind, this body and mind existing from their own side, are projected by ignorance. This temple as something real from its own side, something concrete and independent, is projected from our mind, from the imprint left by our past ignorance. True existence is decorated on the merely labeled temple and that's how it becomes a concrete temple. The appearance of that concrete temple is a hallucination—it doesn't exist. The temple exists but what is that temple that exists? The merely labeled temple exists but the concrete temple doesn't. This unlabeled, concrete, real temple from its own side is decorated, or projected there, and that is a hallucination.

It is the same with any object that we see. When we see a flower, we see a concrete flower, something real from its own side. Again, that is a hallucination. The real flower from its own side is projected, or decorated, onto the merely labeled flower by the imprint left on our mind by the ignorance believing in true existence. On the mere flower, we put a truly existent flower.

We decorate all these concrete things, all these truly existent things, on all the merely labeled things. We put true existence on everything. We decorate everything, which is merely labeled, with true existence. We cover everything with true existence. This hallucination is projected by the mind, by the imprint left by ignorance. This temple doesn't exist from its own side; it doesn't exist independently. The truly existent car, the real car from its own side, doesn't exist; it's completely empty. The real I from its own side, the real car from its own side, the real road from its own side, the real house from its own side, the real shop from its own side—in reality all these things are completely empty. What exists is what is merely imputed—only that. You can now see how things are empty in reality.

How to meditate on emptiness

The way to meditate is to look at the I. Even though it appears to be a real one from its own side, this is a projection. Think, "This is a projection. This truly existent I is projected onto the mere I by my mind, by the imprint left by ignorance." Be aware that this real I, this truly existent I, is a hallucination. Think, "This is the object to be refuted." A truly existent I appears to you, but in your heart you're aware that this is the object to be refuted. This is a projection of the imprint left by the hallucinated mind of ignorance. The point is to recognize that this is a hallucination and is the object to be refuted. When your mind thinks, "This is a hallucination," the thought comes that in reality the I is empty.

It's the same with any external object that you see. When you see a table, it appears to be something completely real from its own side, but this is a hallucination, the object to be refuted. In reality it is not there. When you look at a flower, think, "This real flower appearing from its own side is a projection, a hallucination. In reality, there's no such thing there."

If you practice mindfulness of how everything that appears to exist from its own side is a hallucination, you're always practicing awareness of emptiness. It naturally becomes awareness of emptiness. The more objects you look at, the more you're aware of emptiness; the more names you think of, the more you're aware of emptiness; the more objects you see or have, the more meditation on emptiness you do. Meditating like this becomes very powerful, very effective meditation on emptiness.

You can now see how big a difference there is between your life and reality. It's like the difference between earth and sky. How you live your life, how you create things and believe in them, is completely contrary to reality, which is emptiness.

Dedication

Think, "Due to all the empty merits of the three times—past, present and future—accumulated by me and by all other beings, may the empty I achieve the empty enlightenment and lead the empty sentient beings to that empty enlightenment."

Dedicate the merits with awareness of what I have just described about the hallucination. This way of dedicating is pure, in the sense of being unstained by the concept of true existence. This merit can't later be destroyed by anger or wrong views.

It's very important to know how to dedicate merit. Otherwise, even though you put so much effort into the motivation and the actual action of accumulating merit, if the dedication is not done correctly, your merit can be destroyed by anger or wrong views.

Great Enlightenment Temple, New York
8 September 1990

· · · 4 · · ·

Different Ways of Looking at Things

Do not commit any non-virtuous actions,
Perform only perfect virtuous actions,
Subdue your mind thoroughly—
This is the teaching of the Buddha.

Meditation on impermanence and emptiness

LOOK AT SELF, ACTION, object, friend, enemy, stranger, body and possessions—all these things are transitory in nature, changing within every second by causes and conditions. They are not definite, in the sense that you can always have them, that they will always last. Therefore, there's no basis to give rise to anger, the dissatisfied mind of desire, the concept of permanence and other wrong concepts.

Everything—what is called "I," "action" and "object," the names that we say and hear—is labeled. When we talk, we talk by labeling on a base. From morning to night, everything we think, talk or hear about is labeled. We think things that we have labeled. We talk about things that we have labeled. We hear things that we have labeled.

Everything, every word, shows that it is empty of existing from its own side. Everything, every word, shows that it is a dependent arising, merely imputed by the mind in dependence upon its base. Everything is like this. The way each of these things exists is by being merely imputed by the mind in dependence upon its base.

Since every single thing that we think, say or hear is a dependent arising, everything is empty of existing from its own side. I, action, object, sense objects, samsara and nirvana, true suffering and true cause of suffering, true cessation of suffering and true path—everything is empty of existing from its own side.

Be aware that all these things—I, action, object, all the five sense objects, samsara, nirvana, true suffering, true cause of suffering, true cessation, true path—are empty. One-pointedly concentrate on them, looking at their nature, which is empty. This is the way to meditate on *The Essence of Wisdom*,[17] the essence of the entire Buddhadharma and especially of all the teachings of the *Prajnaparamita*, the Wisdom Gone Beyond.

The way things exist is by being merely imputed by the mind. That's all. True existence is decorated, or projected, onto the merely labeled I, merely labeled actions, merely labeled objects, merely labeled true suffering and true cause of suffering, merely labeled true cessation of suffering and true path. It is because true existence is projected onto all these things that they appear concrete or real, in the sense of having existence from their own side. Starting with the real I, all these things that appear to have existence from their own side, to be

[17] The *Heart Sutra*; see the appendix of this book.

unlabeled, independent, are hallucinations. The true existence of all these things is projected by our own mind, by our ignorance, and these truly existent things are all hallucinations.

Believing that the way these things appear is true blocks our seeing their reality, emptiness only (Skt: *shunyata*; Tib: *tong-pa-nyid*).[18]

Concentrate on this for a little while, starting with the real I that is appearing from its own side. Focus your mind on your perception of things as real, as having existence from their own side. Then think, "All these appearances are projected by ignorance, by the concept of true existence. They are all hallucinations." Apply the word "hallucination" to these things, then meditate on the meaning of hallucination in relation to what you perceive, to what appears to you. Recognize what the hallucination is and think of the meaning of hallucination. Concentrate intensely on this.

Looking at the hallucination

We can also look at things with our eyes open and meditate on the meaning of hallucination. In reality, every form is merely imputed but it doesn't appear to us in that way; it appears to have existence from its own side, to be an independent, real form. With your eyes open, look at a form and think, "This is a projection of my ignorance. This is a hallucination." While looking at things with your eyes open, meditate on the meaning of hallucination.

---

[18] The *only*, not usually used in the English expression, emphasizes that it is the lack of true existence that is being referred to rather than ordinary emptiness, as in empty space.

Recognize the object to be refuted. Look at what is appearing to you. Looking at an object means looking at your perception of it, at what appears to your mind. There's no object that exists other than that which appears to your mind. It is the view of your own mind. Looking at an object means looking at your own view of it, which is the production of your present level, or quality, of mind. How purely or impurely you see an object has completely to do with the quality of your mind, whether it is pure or impure. And this applies to how you see everything: people, buildings, holy objects and so forth.

Looking at an object means looking at a creation of your own mind. A form is something that has color and shape and can be seen by the eye. There are different definitions of form. Sounds, smells, tastes and tangible objects are all also classified as forms, but here we're talking about the particular form that is an object of the eye-sense.

Generally, "form" is labeled on something that has color and shape, is substantial and is an object of the eye-sense. Even though that is the reality of form, form doesn't appear as merely imputed. Form appears as having true existence, existence from its own side. A cover of true existence is projected by ignorance onto the mere form. So while you are looking at things, think, "This is a projection of my ignorance. This is a hallucination." Without closing your eyes, look at things and meditate on the meaning of hallucination.

Look at what it is that doesn't exist and what it is that does. If you can't differentiate between them, ask yourself, "How do things appear to me? Does this form appear to me to be labeled or unlabeled?" If it appears to you to be unlabeled, that is a hallucination, because no unlabeled form exists. If it's a form it has to be labeled "form" by the mind. That's the only way that it can exist. If it appears to be unlabeled, that means it's a hallucination. You then meditate on the meaning of hallucination.

Like a dream

Another easy way to meditate on emptiness is to think, "This is a dream." This might make it easier to understand how these truly existent forms—you the meditator, the building, the lights—are empty. To feel the emptiness you look at the forms of the building or the lights as things in a dream. To feel the emptiness of the building, the lights, and all these other things that appear to be real forms from their own side, look at them and label, "This is a dream and I am dreaming. I am dreaming that I'm in the Great Enlightenment Temple in New York. I am dreaming that I'm seeing all these statues, altars, lights, buildings and people."

To feel the emptiness label, "I am dreaming." It's as if you are dreaming but the difference is that you recognize the dream as a dream. You should understand "This is a dream" to mean that these things don't exist. This is not saying that you the meditator, the building, the lights and the altar don't exist, but that these things that appear to be more than what is merely imputed don't exist. Trying to see that these truly existent things are empty is the main point. You are trying to see the truly existent meditator and other truly existent forms, which are empty, as empty.

In the view of the conventional, or all-obscuring, mind, in the view of ignorance, this is a building, this is a light and this is an altar. Even though they are all labeled, or merely imputed, they appear to be unlabeled, to exist from their own side. True existence is projected onto the mere I and everything else. Even though everything exists in mere name, it is covered by true existence projected by the imprint left by ignorance on our mental continuum. In reality all these are hallucinations. In reality everything is completely empty.

In emptiness there's no such thing as you and I. In emptiness there's no such thing as this and that. In emptiness there's nothing. In emptiness there's no samsara, no liberation, no hell, no enlightenment, no negative karma, no good karma. In emptiness there's no gain, no loss. In emptiness there's no gaining a friend, no losing a friend.

Such things exist only in the view of the obscuring mind, by labeling "gain" and "loss," by labeling "gaining a friend" and "losing a friend," by labeling "enlightenment" and "hell," by labeling "liberation" and "samsara," by labeling "virtue" and "nonvirtue."

In emptiness there's no east and west. In emptiness there's no I and no he or she, another separate person. In emptiness there is no here and there.

It might be useful to meditate this way when you have a problem in your life. It is a great protection psychologically, stopping depression and also stopping the creation of heavy negative karma.

The I in space

Another way to meditate on emptiness is to think of the I in space. Think that the I, the self, that you feel is in the center of your chest is there in space, having nothing to do with your physical body. Think, "I am there in space."

For most of us, especially as we haven't realized emptiness, the ultimate nature of the I, when we think of the I, we're thinking all the time of the I that doesn't exist, the real I. Because we haven't realized the emptiness of the I, we have no other choice—we can't see or apprehend the mere I. When we think of the I, we think of a real one from its own side, a truly existent one, which doesn't exist.

Think, "I am there in space." Think that what you normally feel in your chest is out there in space. While you are focusing on that I out there in space, which you feel is real, use the logical reasoning, "This I is merely imputed by my mind." Apply this logic right on top of that I. See what the effect is of applying the logic of dependent arising, the king of logic, right on top of that real I.

When you use this logic of dependent arising on the I that you feel to be a real one from its own side, you see that real I become empty. Immediately there's a change in your perception of the I. What appeared before to be a real one from its own side is now empty. It's not there. It is empty right there.

Another logical reasoning you can use on that real I is to think, "This I is not truly existent." This should have the same effect: you see that it is empty. This might also be helpful. This is a little similar to the dharmakaya meditation in the sadhanas of Action Tantra, such as nyung-nä, or of Highest Yoga Tantra. This meditation can actually be helpful for that.

You can also do the same meditation wherever you feel the I is in your body—in your brain, your chest, your channels and chakras or somewhere else. Using this logical reasoning, you can analyze whether or not this I exists. If, by using this reasoning, you find that it doesn't exist, you then see that it's empty.

If the I really were in a particular location in your body or in your mind, as you feel it to be, it would mean the I is truly existent. In that case there would be no way you could use the logic of dependent arising because it wouldn't be a dependent arising. In other words, if there were an I located somewhere in the body, in the mind or in the association of both the body and mind, if the I that appears to us were true, it would mean that the I is truly existent. If the I were able to be found somewhere, it would mean that it is truly existent. If the I were truly existent there would be no way to apply the logic of dependent arising to it because it wouldn't exist in that way.

By analyzing in that way, you should be able to find the I. But in reality, while at the beginning it looks as if you should be able to find it, as soon as you start to logically analyze whether or not it exists as it appears to exist, it immediately becomes unclear. What appears to be a real I from its own side immediately becomes unclear as soon as you apply the logic of dependent arising to it. As you analyze more and more, the real I from its own side becomes more and more unclear. This proves that there's no such I. There's no such I on or inside this body, on the consciousness, or even on the whole group of these aggregates. This I is nowhere. It proves that such an I is nowhere on these aggregates.

Wrong conventional truth

The mind of a worldly being, someone who hasn't realized emptiness, can discriminate between correct conventional truth and wrong conventional truth. However, the mind of a worldly being can't recognize the object to be refuted, that things that appear to exist from their own side are hallucinations.

As I mentioned earlier,[19] the Middle Way teachings give the following example to describe the different views. A magician uses mantric power or the power of substances to transform a jewel palace or a beautiful man or woman. The people in the audience, whose eye-senses are made defective by the power of mantras or substances, don't know that what they see is a transformation by the magician, so they believe that what appears to them is real. The same things appear to the eye-sense of the magician, but he has no belief that they are real. A third person doesn't see the hallucination at all because his mind is not affected by the power of mantras or substances. There are these three categories of people.

The members of the audience can later find out that their concept was wrong, that what they saw was a hallucination, the magician's transformation.

In the view of worldly beings, the I, aggregates and sense objects, which exist in mere name, appear to exist from their own side and they believe this to be true. In their view, things having existence from their own side is correct conventional truth.

[19] See p. 43 ff.

Now, arya beings have the wisdom that directly sees, or realizes, that since all these things are merely imputed, they are empty of existing from their own side. However, when they are not in equipoise meditation on emptiness, even though things appear to them as having existence from their own side, these transcendent beings who have the wisdom directly perceiving everything as empty don't cling to this appearance as true. They have dual view because they still have the imprints left by ignorance that project true existence onto merely labeled things, but they don't cling to that view as true. Like the magician, arya beings see the hallucination but don't believe in it.[20]

Buddhas have completely purified even the subtle hallucinations, the subtle obscurations, the imprints left on the mental continuum by ignorance, the concept of true existence.

In the view of worldly beings' minds, things that are labeled appear to be unlabeled, to have existence from their own side. They regard this view as correct.

Because of fever or liver disease, people can see a white snow mountain as yellow or because of wind disease, as blue. Because his senses have been affected by drugs, someone can think that there are a lot of people talking even though there's nobody else in the house. After eating datura, people can see the whole ground as full of worms. Worldly beings can see that these views are wrong, that they don't exist in reality. They see that there is wrong conventional truth and right conventional truth.

[20] Because of recording problems, forty-five minutes of the teaching were missed at this point.

But in the view of higher beings, those who have realized emptiness, everything that appears to the mind of a worldly being is wrong;
it is all wrong conventional truth. In the view of arya beings, everything that appears to a worldly being's mind is mistaken. It is also
mistaken to view things as having existence from their own side, or
inherent existence; it's a wrong conventional truth. Worldly beings
discriminate right and wrong, but in the view of arya beings, everything that appears to the minds of worldly beings is wrong.

Great Enlightenment Temple, New York
9 September 1990

··· 5 ···

Merely Labeled

Recognizing the object to be refuted

To us, THIS I always appears inherently existent, or real. Everything always appears inherently existent. Everything always appears as the object to be refuted. Even saying "this I" is enough to make the object to be refuted appear. We don't need to describe true existence or anything else. For most of us, when we simply say "I," what appears to us, and what we believe it to be, is the truly existent I.

The aggregate of form is not this I, the aggregate of feeling is not this I, the aggregate of recognition is not this I, the compounding aggregates are not this I and the aggregate of consciousness is not this I. The term *compounding aggregates,* or compositional mental factors, refers to all the fifty-one mental factors[21] apart from feeling and recognition. What they compound is their own result, their own continuation. For example, since today's consciousness produces tomorrow's consciousness, it compounds the result, tomorrow's consciousness.

---

[21] For a description of the fifty-one mental factors, see *Meditation on Emptiness,* pp. 238–68.

Even the whole group of the five aggregates is not the I because it is the base to be labeled "I." This makes it clear that it is not the I. The I exists nowhere on these aggregates, neither on the body nor on the mind nor even on the whole group of the aggregates. This is a clear way to meditate on emptiness, enabling us to understand the base and the label.

However, this doesn't mean that there's no I. There is I. The reason there's I is that there are the aggregates, the association of body and mind. Simply because of that, we believe that there's I.

Another way to meditate on emptiness is to ask yourself, "What am I doing now?" You reply, "I'm sitting." Then ask yourself, "Why do I say that I'm sitting?" "There's no other reason at all to believe that I'm sitting except that my body is doing the action of sitting." And when you say, "I'm thinking" or "I'm listening to teachings," why do you believe you're thinking or listening to teachings? There's no other reason at all except that your mind is thinking or listening to teachings.

This way of meditating helps us to recognize the object to be refuted. It is only because the aggregates are sitting, standing, eating, drinking or sleeping that we believe "I'm sitting," "I'm standing," "I'm eating," "I'm drinking" or "I'm sleeping." The I is merely imputed in dependence upon the aggregates and the actions of the aggregates.

With this reasoning, there's suddenly a big change in your view of the I. The concrete I, the real I, suddenly becomes empty right there. The real I from its own side that appeared before is not there. When you don't think of this reasoning, everything comes back, and the I, which is merely imputed, appears as real.

Analyzing the nature of the I by using the reason of the existence of the aggregates and its actions helps us to see more and more clearly what the emotional I is. The I that appears to be real from its own side is completely empty; it doesn't exist. When your mind becomes distracted, look again at how the I appears and apply the reasoning. When you analyze, again you won't find that real I, that emotional I. Not being able to find the emotional I is a sign that it doesn't exist.

You are unable to find the I on these aggregates. None of these aggregates is the I and on these aggregates there's no I. But that doesn't mean that the I doesn't exist. The I exists. There is I in this temple. During this time that the aggregates are in this temple, we believe "I am here in this temple." Just by that, we believe "I am in this temple." And we believe "I'm listening" or "I'm talking"—or "I'm feeling tired" or "I'm sleeping" as this never-ending talk goes on and on!

Recognizing the hallucination

The different meditations I have mentioned can be used to meditate on emptiness, to see the nature of the I. Look at how things appear to you. They appear as real, as existing from their own side. The most important point is to then think that this is a hallucination, a projection. A camera records various activities, such as fighting, and if you have power and a projector you can then project the film onto a screen. But what you see there on the screen is not real. You might see thousands of people fighting on a TV screen but there's nobody really there on the screen. What appears is not real; it's not true. Exactly like a camera recording images on a film, ignorance leaves imprints on our mental continuum and we then project true existence onto the things we experience.

The main point to meditate on is that the projection of true existence is a hallucination. When you think of hallucination, the understanding should come in your heart that these things are empty; they don't exist. It's not that the building doesn't exist, but the truly existent building, the building that appears to exist from its own side, doesn't exist. That's completely empty. That is the emptiness, or ultimate nature, of the building.

Everything else—self, action, object, all the department stores, the whole city—is also like this. Everything that exists is covered by this hallucination of true existence. When you recognize that it is a hallucination, the understanding should come in your heart that everything is empty. You should then practice awareness of that emptiness. In your everyday life, not only during meditation but also when you're at work, remember again and again to practice this awareness. Look at how things appear to you: they all appear as unlabeled, which means that they are projections, hallucinations. They are empty. You don't have to actually say the word "empty" because when you say that these unlabeled things are hallucinations, the understanding that they are empty naturally arises in your heart.

With this awareness, you can then go shopping. You stand up, put on your shoes and with this awareness go out in your car. When you are walking in the street, you also do it with the recognition that the truly existent things appearing to you are hallucinations. After recognizing that the I that appears to be real is a hallucination, you understand that it is empty. This empty I then walks along the empty street to the empty shops. In reality, everything is like this.

Everything is merely labeled

"I" is merely imputed to these aggregates. None of the five aggregates is the general aggregates. Even the whole group of the five aggregates is not the general aggregates, because it is the base to be labeled "general aggregates." So, "aggregates" is also merely imputed to them.

With respect to the aggregate of form, no part of the body is the aggregate of form and even the whole group of the parts of the body is not the aggregate of form. "Aggregate of form" is merely imputed to this body.

In the same way, each of the aggregates is merely imputed to its own base. For example, "aggregate of consciousness" is merely imputed to the particular mental factor whose main function is to see the essence of an object and which continues from one life to another, carrying the imprints left by karma. That phenomenon is labeled "consciousness."

With respect to the head, the mouth is not the head, the nose is not the head, the brain is not the head, the ears are not the head. No part of the head is the head. Even the whole group of the parts of the head is not the head; it is the base to be labeled "head." Each part of the head—mouth, nose, brain, ear—is merely labeled on another label, and that label is given to another label.

"Arm" is labeled on this particular object, but each part of the arm is not the arm and even the whole group of the parts is not the arm.

Since the whole group is the base to be labeled "arm," it's not the arm. Again, each part is also labeled on another label. It is the same with the leg. Each part of the leg, such as the thigh, is not the leg, and even the whole group of the parts is not the leg. The whole group is the base to be labeled "leg." Each part is labeled on its own base.

This is how it is down to the atoms, and even the atom is labeled. Each particle of the atom is not the atom, and the group of the particles is the base to be labeled "atom." And even the particles of the atoms are labeled on their own base.

From the I and the aggregates down to the atomic particles, everything is labeled on another label. Something is imputed to one base, which is labeled on another base, and that base is labeled on another base. Everything exists being labeled. Everything is a label, starting with our aggregates. So, from the I and the aggregates down to the atomic particles, everything is completely empty of existing from its own side. The concrete things that appear to us are hallucinations. The real, concrete, truly existent I and aggregates are hallucinations.

It is the same with this temple. None of the parts of the temple is the temple. Even the whole group of the parts is not the temple; it is the base to be labeled "temple." So, the temple is completely empty of existing from its own side.

With respect to the ceiling, each part of the ceiling is not the ceiling, and even the whole group of the parts is not the ceiling, because the whole group is the base to be labeled "ceiling." With respect to the windows, each part is not the window, and even the whole group of parts is not the window, because it's the base to be labeled "window."

The reality of the temple, ceiling and windows is something completely different from what we normally think of as the temple, ceiling and windows. When we analyze we find that how they really exist is completely something else. All the time we talk, talk, talk and think, think, think and write, write, write, but when we analyze we find that reality is actually something we have never talked about, never thought about and never written about. It is something that has never appeared to us.

Everything is like this. Even the floor is like this. Each piece of the floor is not the floor, and even the whole group of pieces is not the floor, because they are the base to be labeled "floor." When we again analyze each piece, down to its atoms, it's also the same with the atoms and their particles. Because they are particles *of* the atom, it means the particles are not the atom. And even the whole group of the particles is not the atom; it is the base to be labeled "atom." So, from the temple down to its atoms, everything is labeled. We put one label on this label and then put another label on that label. We put one name on another name.

Even though this is the reality, what appears to us is a concrete temple with a concrete ceiling, concrete windows and a concrete floor. What appears to us is something existing from its own side. This is a projection by ignorance; this is a hallucination. In reality it's empty.

It is like this from morning until night. We build a house, which is empty, and eat food, which is empty. We marry a wife or husband, who is empty, and have a child, who is empty. We work in an office, which is empty. We get empty money and go to the empty supermarket to buy empty food then go back to our empty house.

The merely labeled I is born from merely labeled parents and goes to a merely labeled school to get a merely labeled education from a merely labeled teacher to get a merely labeled degree, then get a merely labeled job as a merely labeled professor, then marries a merely labeled wife or husband and has a merely labeled child. With merely labeled money, the merely labeled I goes to the merely labeled shop and buys merely labeled things. The merely labeled I wears merely labeled clothes and eats merely labeled food. It is like this from birth to death, from the merely labeled birth to the merely labeled death. The whole thing—beginning with birth and ending with death and everything in between—is merely labeled. This is how it is in reality.

Remembering emptiness in everyday life

Sometimes you might think, "What's the use of teachings on emptiness? How does this philosophy help me when I have problems in everyday life?" However, if you can think like this, it's the most powerful meditation to shatter the hallucinations. It's like an atomic bomb. Problems happen in your daily life because you believe the hallucinations to be real. The most powerful, immediate way to stop problems is to remember emptiness. You should especially remember emptiness when you are in situations where there's a danger of giving rise to strong anger or uncontrolled desire and creating heavy negative karma and causing great harm to others.

When you have a very dissatisfied mind and don't succeed in getting what you want, you experience depression. Even though you might not remember the particular reasons you are depressed, most of the time there are reasons. Depression happens because you didn't succeed in getting what your desire or selfish mind wanted. Depression happens when you not aware of the emptiness of the I and other things. When you are aware of emptiness, when you're meditating on emptiness, there's no depression. There's no way depression can be there at that time. Depression happens when you believe the hallucinations to be real.

It is especially important to remember emptiness in those situations in your daily life that create a lot of confusion, where there is danger of great harm to you and other sentient beings. It is very important to remember that the things that look real from their own side are projections, hallucinations. Then meditate strongly that they are empty.

One way to meditate on how everything is empty is to meditate on dependent arising, looking at how everything—self, action, object—is merely imputed. This is one way of practicing awareness of emptiness in everyday life. Do this while you are at work, talking to people or having meetings, or at home with your family. Do it especially when you are having a conversation with someone who is complaining about or criticizing you or when somebody is praising you, which causes the delusion of pride to arise. Again meditate on emptiness; again practice awareness of either dependent arising or emptiness. Anyway, they're the same; it's one meditation.

Fear of losing the I

If fear of losing the I, the self, or external phenomena arises during meditation on emptiness, it's a very good sign, but while bodhisattvas of lower intelligence may feel afraid when experiencing emptiness, when bodhisattvas of higher intelligence realize it, they feel incredible joy, as if they'd found a precious treasure they'd never had before.

If fear arises when you do analysis on emptiness, it means that your connotation of emptiness is hitting the right point, the concept of true existence. It means that your meditation is harming the object that this ignorance apprehends. You mustn't run away from that fear. It's a very good sign; it's what is needed. It's a sign that your meditation is working on the right point. You should experience the fear and go beyond it. If you allow this fear to arise and then go beyond it, you will be able to realize the emptiness of the I without any obstacles. But if you stop the fear when it arises you cannot completely realize the emptiness of the I. This is an extremely important point.

You can experience emptiness with just a little meditation on it at times when you're accumulating much merit and doing intensive purification, and when you have strong devotion to your guru while training your mind in the meditations on seeing your guru as buddha. At such times you can experience it by concentrating on the meaning of just two or three words on emptiness.

So when the fear comes, the most important thing is not to run away from it but to go beyond it. Fear arises because you feel you are losing the I, but in reality there's no way to lose the I because the continuity of consciousness always exists—it goes to enlightenment and always continues. Therefore the I, which is imputed to the consciousness, always exists. There's no way for it to cease. There's no need to worry about falling into the extreme of nihilism, about the I completely ceasing. Even though it appears that you're losing it, there's no need to worry that the I will actually cease.

Feeling that you're losing the I means that you're losing the truly existent I and is the start of seeing the emptiness of the I, its emptiness of true existence. This is a very important point. When you experience complete loss of the I, you see the path of the Madhyamaka, the Middle Way.

You've been holding on to something for beginningless rebirths but when you experience complete loss of the I, suddenly there's nothing to hold on to. Since beginningless time you've been holding on to the false I, the truly existent I, which doesn't exist, and that's why you're still in samsara. As a result, not only have you not achieved enlightenment, as you've been clinging on to the truly existent I, you haven't even achieved liberation, ultimate happiness, for yourself. And you will continue to circle in samsara—in the hell, hungry ghost, animal, human and god realms—until you let it go.

Until you realize emptiness and cut off this ignorance that is the root of samsara, you will have to wander in samsara as you've been doing since beginningless time, continuously experiencing suffering without end, such as the human problems that you experience over and over again.

After you've realized emptiness, if you haven't done so before you should then try to actualize single-pointed concentration. Study the methods of overcoming the distractions of scattering and sinking and establishing concentration.[22] By learning and practicing those techniques you can achieve stable single-pointed concentration. Through this you can then generate great insight and derive the rapturous ecstasy of the extremely refined body and mind that comes from analysis on emptiness.

Everything comes from the mind

Everything comes from our own mind. Since everything is merely imputed and all imputation comes from our mind, everything comes from our mind. All appearances happen by labeling; whatever appears to us happens by labeling. Again, all the appearances of life come from our mind.

The appearance of a friend comes from our mind. Before we label "friend," there's no appearance of friend. Because someone loves us or does something good for us, we label her "friend" and she then appears to us as a friend; because another person doesn't love us or harms us, we label him "enemy" and he then appears to us as an enemy. These appearances come from our own mind. When our enemy appears, an unpleasant feeling arises in our mind; when our friend appears, a pleasant feeling arises in our mind. All this is created by or originates from our own mind.

Without labeling "snake," there's no appearance of snake; after labeling a piece of rope at dusk "snake," a snake appears. It's the same

[22] See, for example, the relevant sections of *The Great Treatise on the Stages of the Path to Enlightenment* or *Liberation in the Palm of Your Hand*.

with a person who doesn't know that George Bush is the president of America. At first she sees just the appearance of a man. After somebody tells her that he's the American president, she then also labels "This is the American president." After she has imputed this and then believed in her own label, the American president then appears to her.

It's like this from morning to night, from birth until death. It's like this with the whole of samsara and nirvana. It's like this with everything that appears to us: with my seeing you and your seeing me and this temple and everything else, including the American president. Everything that appears to us comes from our own mind.

This is also an important point to remember in our daily life, especially when we're in situations where there's a danger of creating confusion and problems and heavy negative karma. If we think like this, there's no way to blame other sentient beings. First we make our own interpretation of a situation and then apply the label "good" or "bad" to it. We label what appears to us as bad, get angry and then blame other people—it's illogical; it doesn't make any sense.

With this reasoning, since everything that appears to us comes from our own mind, we don't find anything for which to blame others. How things appear to us depends on how we look at them, how we interpret them. We then label them.

Hearing that our friend doesn't love us any more is not the problem. We hear that our friend doesn't love us any more and interpret that as bad, but that's still not the problem; labeling that situation "bad," is not the problem. The problem comes when we start to believe in our own label, "This is bad." That's when it becomes a problem and makes our life difficult, not before.

You can see that simply labeling a situation "bad" is not the problem. The problem is that after we label we start to believe in our own label. That's what makes life difficult. Thus you can see how problems like this come from our own mind, are a creation of our own mind.

Produced by ignorance

The ignorance holding the concept of true existence is like a farmer; karma, the action motivated by this ignorance, is like a field in which various types of crops can grow; and consciousness, on which karma leaves all the imprints, is like the seed. One tiny seed carries all the potential to grow a huge tree with many billions of branches that cover a huge area. Like a seed, the consciousness, on which karma left all the imprints, contains all the potential. The consciousness continued from your past life to this life and will continue from this life to your next life, carrying all these imprints.

The imprint left by karma on the consciousness is then made ready to bring its own rebirth, its own future samsara, the aggregates, by craving and grasping, which are like the minerals. That is called becoming, which is like a seed becoming ready to produce its sprout. The next life, or rebirth, starts with name and form, which is like the sprout grown from the seed. After that come the sense bases, contact, feeling, then old age and death.[23]

[23] In the preceding two paragraphs, Rinpoche is describing the twelve links of dependent arising, which illustrate how ignorance is the root of samsara. The twelve links are: ignorance, karma, consciousness, craving, grasping, becoming, rebirth, name and form, the six sense bases, contact, feeling, and aging and death. See The Meaning of Life for a detailed teaching on this topic.

The conclusion is that from morning to night, from birth until death, whatever happiness and suffering we experience and whatever good or bad objects appear to us, they all come from our consciousness, which carries all the imprints. Everything that appears to us from birth until death comes from our own consciousness. All the different experiences we have of people, places and sense objects come from our consciousness, which carries the imprints. It is not only that everything that appears to us today and from birth until death comes from our consciousness but also that the whole appearance of samsara comes from consciousness, which is our own mind. Not only that, but it comes from karma, which is also our own mind. The definition of karma is "the intention arisen from the principal consciousness." So, karma is our own mind. Everything comes from our own mind, from karma. Not only that, but everything that appears to us comes from our own mind, from ignorance.

It is like this with everything in our daily life, including desirable and undesirable objects and people helping or harming us. It all comes from our own mind. Past karma leaves imprints on our consciousness—then, while we're driving comfortably in our car, an accident suddenly happens; or when we step out of our car somebody we've never met before suddenly shoots us for no apparent reason; or while we're walking along the street somebody suddenly appears and beats us up. At such times the imprint left by past karma on our consciousness actualizes, or manifests—it produces the appearance of somebody suddenly shooting or beating us.

It's the same in our family. Whenever somebody is giving us a hard time—scolding, complaining about or beating us—it's all coming

from our own mind. It's very good to remember this when somebody is disrespecting or criticizing us; it's very good to recognize
that it's coming from our consciousness, our own karma, our own
ignorance. This means that there's nothing to get angry about and
nobody else to blame.

It's the same with the sufferings of the hell, hungry ghost and animal realms. The heaviest sufferings of heat in the hot hells and the
heaviest sufferings of hunger and thirst in the hungry ghost realm all
manifest from our consciousness, our karma, our ignorance. They're
all produced by ignorance.

We don't know what karma we have created. Since we can't see
all the karmas we've ever created we can't say that we won't ever
experience leprosy, cancer, AIDS, years of living in a coma or other
serious problems. We can't say for sure that we won't experience the
problems we see others experiencing.

Therefore, it's extremely important to practice Dharma while
you're healthy and possess all the necessary conditions to meditate on
the graduated path to enlightenment. You've met the right path and
qualified masters—and even if you haven't met qualified masters yet,
you still have the opportunity to do so. This is the right time to practice, the right time not to waste your life. This is the time to practice
listening to and reflecting and meditating on the path to enlightenment and to purify negative karma, the cause of suffering. The most
important thing is to try as much as you possibly can to purify the
negative karma accumulated in the past and not to create any more.
You should stop creating negative karma again by taking vows and
living in them. In that way you accumulate merit all the time, purify

past obstacles and do not create further obstacles to developing your mind in the path. Free of obstacles, you then become enlightened and can then guide all sentient beings to enlightenment.

Dedication

Please dedicate the merit [of reading this book] to generating bodhicitta in your mind and in the minds of all sentient beings and to the increase of bodhicitta in the minds of those who have already generated it.

Think, "Due to the merely labeled merits of the three times accumulated by me and others, may the merely labeled I achieve the merely labeled enlightenment and lead the merely labeled sentient beings to that merely labeled enlightenment."

Great Enlightenment Temple, New York
9 September 1990

··· Appendix ···

The Heart of the Perfection of Wisdom Sutra

I prostrate to the Arya Triple Gem.

Thus did I hear at one time. The Bhagavan was dwelling on Mass of Vultures Mountain in Rajagriha together with a great community of monks and a great community of bodhisattvas. At that time, the Bhagavan was absorbed in the concentration on the categories of phenomena called "Profound Perception."

Also, at that time, the bodhisattva mahasattva arya Avalokiteshvara looked upon the very practice of the profound perfection of wisdom and beheld those five aggregates also as empty of inherent nature.

Then, through the power of Buddha, the venerable Shariputra said this to the bodhisattva mahasattva arya Avalokiteshvara: "How should any son of the lineage train who wishes to practice the activity of the profound perfection of wisdom?"

He said that, and the bodhisattva mahasattva arya Avalokiteshvara said this to the venerable Sharadvatiputra. "Shariputra, any son of the lineage or daughter of the lineage who wishes to practice the activity of the profound perfection of wisdom should look upon it like this, correctly and repeatedly beholding those five aggregates also as empty of inherent nature.

"Form is empty. Emptiness is form. Emptiness is not other than form; form is also not other than emptiness. In the same way, feeling, discrimination, compositional factors and consciousness are empty.

"Shariputra, likewise, all phenomena are emptiness; without characteristic; unproduced, unceased; stainless, not without stain; not deficient, not fulfilled.

"Shariputra, therefore, in emptiness there is no form, no feeling, no discrimination, no compositional factors, no consciousness; no eye, no ear, no nose, no tongue, no body, no mind; no visual form, no sound, no odor, no taste, no object of touch and no phenomenon. There is no eye element and so on up to and including no mind element and no mental consciousness element. There is no ignorance, no extinction of ignorance and so on up to and including no aging and death and no extinction of aging and death. Similarly, there is no suffering, origination, cessation and path; there is no exalted wisdom, no attainment and also no non-attainment.

"Shariputra, therefore, because there is no attainment, bodhisattvas rely on and dwell in the perfection of wisdom, the mind without obscuration and without fear. Having completely passed beyond error, they reach the end-point of nirvana. All the buddhas who dwell in the three times also manifestly, completely awaken to unsurpassable, perfect, complete enlightenment in reliance on the perfection of wisdom.

"Therefore, the mantra of the perfection of wisdom, the mantra of great knowledge, the unsurpassed mantra, the mantra equal to the unequaled, the mantra that thoroughly pacifies all suffering, should be known as truth since it is not false. The mantra of the perfection of wisdom is declared: TADYATHA [OM] GATE GATE PARAGATE PARA-SAMGATE BODHI SVAHA

"Shariputra, the bodhisattva mahasattva should train in the profound perfection of wisdom like that."

Then the Bhagavan arose from that concentration and commended the bodhisattva mahasattva arya Avalokiteshvara saying: "Well said, well said, son of the lineage, it is like that. It is like that; one should practice the profound perfection of wisdom just as you have indicated; even the tathagatas rejoice."

The Bhagavan having thus spoken, the venerable Sharadvatiputra, the bodhisattva mahasattva arya Avalokiteshvara, those surrounding in their entirety along with the world of gods, humans, asuras and gandharvas were overjoyed and highly praised that spoken by the Bhagavan.

Colophon:

Translated from the Tibetan, consulting the Indian and Tibetan commentaries and previous good translations, by Gelong Thubten Tsultrim (George Churinoff), the first day of Saka Dawa, 1999, at Tushita Meditation Centre, Dharamsala, India. Amended March 8, 2001 in the New Mexico desert.

··· Bibliography ···

FPMT Education Department. *Essential Buddhist Prayers*. Portland: FPMT, 2006.

Gyatso, Tenzin, His Holiness the Dalai Lama. *The Meaning of Life*. Boston: Wisdom Publication, 1992.

Hopkins, Jeffrey. *Meditation on Emptiness*. Boston: Wisdom Publications, 1983.

Pabongka Rinpoche. *Liberation in the Palm of Your Hand*. Boston: Wisdom Publications, 1991.

Rabten, Geshe, and Geshe Ngawang Dhargyey. *Advice from a Spiritual Friend*. Boston: Wisdom Publications, 1977 and 1996.

Tegchok, Geshe Jampa. *The Kindness of Others*. Lama Yeshe Wisdom Archive, 2006.

Tsongkhapa, Lama Je. *The Great Treatise on the Stages of the Path to Enlightenment*. Ithaca: Snow Lion Publications, 2000–4.

Zopa Rinpoche, Lama Thubten. *The Joy of Compassion*. Boston: Lama Yeshe Wisdom Archive, 2006.

———. *Transforming Problems into Happiness*. Boston: Wisdom Publications, 2001.

··· Glossary ···

(*Skt = Sanskrit; Tib = Tibetan.*)

Action Tantra (*Skt: Kriya Tantra*). The first of the four classes of tantra, which mainly emphasizes external activities.

aggregates. The association of body and mind. A person comprises five aggregates: form, feeling, recognition, compositional factors and consciousness.

altruism. See *bodhicitta.*

anger. A disturbing thought that exaggerates the negative qualities of an object and wishes to harm it; one of the six root delusions. See also *delusions.*

arya being. A being who has directly realized emptiness.

asura (*Skt*). Or demigod. A being in the god realms who enjoys greater comfort and pleasure than human beings, but who suffers from jealousy and quarreling.

Atisha, Lama (982–1054). The great Indian teacher who first formulated the lam-rim when he came to Tibet in 1042.

attachment. A disturbing thought that exaggerates the positive qualities of an object and wishes to possess it; one of the six root delusions. See also *delusions.*

bodhicitta (*Skt*). The altruistic determination to achieve enlightenment for the sole purpose of enlightening all sentient beings.

buddhahood. See *enlightenment.*

buddha-nature. Refers to the emptiness, or ultimate nature, of the mind. Because of this nature, every sentient being possesses the potential to become fully enlightened.

buddha (*Skt*). A fully enlightened being. One who has purified all obscurations of the mind and perfected all good qualities. See also *enlightenment*, *Shakyamuni Buddha*.

compassion. The sincere wish that others be free from suffering and its causes.

Compassion Buddha (*Skt: Avalokiteshvara; Tib: Chenrezig*). A male meditational deity embodying the compassion of all the buddhas. The Dalai Lamas are said to be emanations of this deity.

compounding aggregates. Or compositional factors. This aggregate includes all the other factors of a person not included in the four aggregates of form, feeling, recognition and consciousness.

consciousness. The aggregate of consciousness includes mental consciousness as well as the various types of sensory consciousness. See also *mind*.

conventional truth. Relative truth; the way things appear to exist as distinct from the way in which they actually exist; what is true for a valid mind not perceiving ultimate truth.

cyclic existence. See *samsara*.

defilements. See *obscurations*.

delusions. The negative thoughts that are the cause of suffering. The three root delusions are ignorance, anger and attachment; also called the three poisons.

dependent arising. The way that the self and phenomena exist conventionally as relative and interdependent. They come into existence in dependence upon (1) causes and conditions, (2) their parts, and, most subtly, (3) the mind imputing, or labeling, them.

desire. See *attachment*.

deva (*Skt*). A god dwelling in a state with much comfort and pleasure in the desire, form or formless realms.

Dharma (*Skt*). In general, spiritual practice; specifically, the teachings of Buddha, which protect from suffering and lead to liberation and full enlightenment.

dharmakaya (*Skt*). The omniscient mind of a buddha.

disturbing thoughts. See *delusions*.

emptiness (*Skt: shunyata*). The lack of the apparent independent self-existence of phenomena.

enlightenment. Full awakening; buddhahood. A state characterized by infinite wisdom, or omniscience; infinite compassion; and perfect power.

Essence of Wisdom. Also known as *The Heart Sutra;* see the appendix of this book. Recited daily by many Buddhist practitioners, it is one of the shortest of the *Perfection of Wisdom* texts. See also *Prajnaparamita*.

feeling. The aggregate of feeling includes feelings of pleasure, pain and neutrality.

form. The aggregate of form includes all objects of the five senses (sight, smell, hearing, taste and touch), as well as the four elements (earth, water, fire and air).

form realm. The second of samsara's three realms, with seventeen classes of gods.

formless realm. The highest of samsara's three realms, with four classes of gods involved in formless meditations: infinite space, infinite consciousness, nothingness and the peak of cyclic existence.

four noble truths. True suffering, true cause of suffering, true cessation of suffering and true path; the four characteristics of conditioned existence seen to be true by an *arya* being. The subject of Shakyamuni Buddha's first teaching.

god. See *deva*.

great compassion. Taking personal responsibility for freeing sentient beings from suffering and its causes.

great insight. The meditative understanding of impermanence and emptiness that overcomes ignorance and leads to liberation.

Great Vehicle. See *Mahayana*.

guru (*Skt; Tib: lama*). Literally, heavy, as in heavy with Dharma knowledge. A spiritual teacher, master.

hell. The samsaric realm with the greatest suffering.

Highest Yoga Tantra. The highest of the four classes of tantra, which mainly emphasizes internal activities.

hungry ghost (*Skt: preta*). One of the six classes of samsaric beings, hungry ghosts experience the greatest sufferings of hunger and thirst.

ignorance. A mental factor that obscures and confuses the mind from seeing the way in which things exist in reality. There are basically two types of ignorance, ignorance of karma and the ignorance that holds the concept of true existence, the fundamental delusion from which all other delusions arise. See also *delusions.*

impermanence. The gross and subtle levels of the transience of phenomena.

imprints. The seeds, or potentials, left on the mind by positive or negative actions of body, speech and mind.

inherent existence. See *true existence.*

karma (*Skt*). Literally, action. The working of cause and effect, whereby positive actions produce happiness and negative actions produce suffering.

lam-rim (*Tib*). The graduated path to enlightenment. A presentation of Shakyamuni Buddha's teachings as step-by-step training for a disciple to achieve enlightenment. See also *Atisha.*

liberation. The state of complete liberation from samsara; the goal of a practitioner seeking their own freedom from suffering.

loving kindness. The wish for others to have happiness and its causes.

Madhyamaka (*Skt*). See *Middle Way.*

Mahayana (*Skt*). Literally, Great Vehicle. The path of the bodhisattvas, those seeking enlightenment in order to enlighten all other beings.

Manjushri (*Skt*). A male meditational deity embodying the wisdom of all the buddhas.

mantra (*Skt*). Literally, mind protection. Mantras are Sanskrit syllables usually recited in conjunction with the practice of a particular meditational deity and embodying the qualities of that deity.

Marpa (1012–1096). A great Tibetan Buddhist translator; a founding figure of the Kagyu tradition and root guru of Milarepa.

meditation. Familiarization of the mind with a virtuous object. There are two main types of meditation: analytical and concentration.

merely labeled. The subtlest meaning of dependent arising; every phenomenon exists relatively, or conventionally, as a mere label, merely imputed by the mind.

merit. The positive energy accumulated in the mind as a result of virtuous actions of body, speech and mind. The principal cause of happiness. See also *virtue.*

method. All aspects of the path to enlightenment other than those associated with the development of the realization of emptiness, principally love, compassion and bodhicitta.

Middle Way (*Skt*: *Madhyamaka*). A philosophical system founded by Nagarjuna, based on the *Perfection of Wisdom Sutras* of Shakyamuni Buddha, and considered to be the supreme presentation of Buddha's teachings on emptiness.

Milarepa (1040–1123). A great Tibetan yogi famed for his impeccable relationship with his guru, Marpa, his asceticism, and his songs of realization. A founding figure of the Kagyu tradition.

mind. Synonymous with consciousness. Defined as "that which is clear and knowing"; a formless entity that has the ability to perceive objects. Mind is divided into six primary consciousnesses and fifty-one mental factors.

Nagarjuna (*Skt*). The second century CE Indian Buddhist philosopher who propounded the Madhyamaka philosophy of emptiness.

nihilism. The mistaken view that nothing exists.

nirvana (*Skt*). See *liberation.*

nonvirtue. Negative karma; that which results in suffering.

nyung-nä (Tib). A two-day retreat, involving prostrations, fasting and silence, related to Thousand-Arm Chenrezig, Buddha of Compassion.

object to be refuted. The true existence of the I and other phenomena.

obscurations. Defilements that obscure the mind. There are two divisions: disturbing-thought obscurations, which obstruct the attainment of liberation, and the more subtle obscurations to omniscience, which obstruct the attainment of enlightenment.

oral transmission (Tib: lung). The verbal transmission of a teaching, meditation practice or mantra from guru to disciple, the guru having received the transmission in an unbroken lineage from the original source.

perfect human rebirth. The rare human state, qualified by eight freedoms and ten richnesses, which is the ideal condition for practicing Dharma and attaining enlightenment.

pervasive compounding suffering. The most subtle of the three types of suffering, it refers to the nature of the five aggregates, which are contaminated by karma and delusions.

Prajnaparamita (Skt). Or, in English, *Perfection of Wisdom.* The teachings of Shakyamuni Buddha in which the wisdom of emptiness and the path of the bodhisattva are explained.

Prasangika (Skt). The Middle Way Consequence School; considered to the highest of all Buddhist philosophical tenets. The second division of the *Madhyamaka*, one of the four schools of Buddhist philosophy.

recognition. The aggregate of recognition is the mental factor that allows us to distinguish one thing or event from another.

renunciation. The state of mind not having the slightest attraction to samsaric perfections for even a second and having the strong wish for liberation.

Rinpoche (Tib). Literally, precious one. Generally, a title given to a lama who has intentionally taken rebirth in a human body to continue helping others. A respectful title used for one's own lama.

sadhana (Skt). Method of accomplishment; meditational and mantra practices associated with a particular deity, often performed as a daily practice.

samsara (*Skt*). Cyclic existence; the six realms: the lower realms of the hell beings, hungry ghosts and animals, and the upper realms of the humans, demigods and gods; the recurring cycle of death and rebirth within one or other of the six realms. It also refers to the contaminated aggregates of a sentient being.

self-cherishing. The self-centered attitude of considering one's own happiness to be more important that that of others; the main obstacle to the realization of bodhicitta.

sentient being. Any unenlightened being; any being whose mind is not completely free from ignorance.

Shakyamuni Buddha (563–483 BC). The founder of the present Buddhadharma. Fourth of the one thousand founding buddhas of this present world age, he was born a prince of the Shakya clan in north India and taught the sutra and tantra paths to liberation and full enlightenment.

shamatha (*Skt*). Calm abiding; a state of concentration in which the mind is able to abide steadily, without effort and for as long as desired, on an object of meditation.

shunyata (*Skt*). See *emptiness.*

six paramitas (*Skt*). Or six perfections. The practices of a bodhisattva: charity, morality, patience, enthusiastic perseverance, concentration and wisdom.

six root delusions. Ignorance, anger, attachment, pride, jealousy and wrong views.

subtle dependent arising. See *merely labeled.*

suffering. See *true suffering.*

sura (*Skt*). A being in the god realm that enjoys the highest pleasures to be found in cyclic existence.

sutra (*Skt*). The open discourses of Shakyamuni Buddha; a scriptural text and the teachings and practices it contains.

Svatantrika. The Middle Way Autonomy School; the first division of the *Madhyamaka,* one of the four schools of Buddhist philosophy.

tantra (*Skt*). The secret teachings of the Buddha; a scriptural text and the teachings and practices it contains.

Tara (*Skt*). A female meditational deity that embodies the enlightened activity of all the buddhas; often referred to as the mother of the buddhas of the past, present, and future.

thought transformation (*Tib: lo-jong*). A powerful approach to the development of bodhicitta, in which the mind is trained to use all situations, both happy and unhappy, as a means to destroy self-cherishing and self-grasping.

true cause of suffering. The second of the four noble truths, it refers to karma and delusion.

true cessation of suffering. The third of the four noble truths, it is the state of liberation from suffering and the true causes of suffering.

true existence. The type of concrete, real existence from its own side that everything appears to possess; in fact, everything is empty of true existence.

true path. The fourth noble truth, it refers to the methods of Dharma practice that lead sentient beings to the true cessation of suffering.

true suffering. The first of the four noble truths, it refers to the fact that all conditioned existence is pervaded by suffering. There are three levels: suffering of suffering, changeable suffering and all-pervasive suffering.

Tsongkhapa, Lama (1357–1419). The revered teacher and accomplished practitioner who founded the Gelug order of Tibetan Buddhism.

ultimate nature. See *ultimate truth.*

ultimate truth. The way things actually exist as distinct from how they appear to exist; emptiness; the absence of inherent existence.

Vajrapani (*Skt*). A wrathful male meditational deity embodying the power of all the buddhas.

Vajrasattva (*Skt*). A male meditational deity used as the object of concentration in certain purification practices.

virtue. Positive karma; that which results in happiness. See also *merit.*

wind disease (Tib: *lung*). The state in which the wind element within the body is unbalanced.

wisdom. All aspects of the path to enlightenment associated with the development of the realization of emptiness.

Yeshe, Lama (1935–1984). Born and educated in Tibet, he fled the Chinese occupation in 1959 and continued his study and practice in India, where he met his chief disciple, Lama Zopa Rinpoche. They began teaching Westerners at Kopan Monastery in 1974 and founded the Foundation for the Preservation of the Mahayana Tradition in 1975.

LAMA YESHE WISDOM ARCHIVE

The LAMA YESHE WISDOM ARCHIVE (LYWA) is the collected works of Lama Thubten Yeshe and Lama Thubten Zopa Rinpoche. The ARCHIVE was founded in 1996 by Lama Zopa Rinpoche, its spiritual director, to make available in various ways the teachings it contains. Publication of books of edited teachings for free distribution is one of the ways.

Lama Yeshe and Lama Zopa Rinpoche began teaching at Kopan Monastery, Nepal, in 1970. Since then, their teachings have been recorded and transcribed. At present we have more than 10,000 hours of digital audio and some 60,000 pages of raw transcript on our computers. Many recordings, mostly teachings by Lama Zopa Rinpoche, remain to be transcribed, and as Rinpoche continues to teach, the number of recordings in the ARCHIVE increases accordingly. Most of our transcripts have been neither checked nor edited.

Here at the LYWA we are making every effort to organize the transcription of that which has not yet been transcribed, edit that which has not yet been edited, and generally do the many other tasks detailed below. In all this, we need your financial help. Please contact us for more information:

LAMA YESHE WISDOM ARCHIVE
PO Box 356, Weston, MA 02493, USA
Telephone (781) 259-4466; Fax (678) 868-4806
info@LamaYeshe.com
www.LamaYeshe.com

THE ARCHIVE TRUST

The work of the LAMA YESHE WISDOM ARCHIVE falls into two categories: archiving and dissemination.

Archiving requires managing the recordings of teachings by Lama Yeshe and Lama Zopa Rinpoche that have already been collected, collecting recordings of teachings given but not yet sent to the ARCHIVE, and collecting recordings of Lama Zopa's on-going teachings, talks, advice and so forth as he travels the world for the benefit of all. Incoming media are then catalogued and stored safely while being kept accessible for further work.

We organize the transcription of audio, add the transcripts to the already existent database of teachings, manage this database, have transcripts checked, and make transcripts available to editors or others doing research on or practicing these teachings.

Other archiving activities include working with video and photographs of the Lamas and digitizing ARCHIVE materials.

Dissemination involves making the Lamas' teachings available through various avenues including books for free distribution, books for sale through Wisdom Publications, lightly edited transcripts, a monthly e-letter (see below), audio CDs, DVDs, articles in *Mandala* and other magazines and on our Web site. Irrespective of the medium we choose, the teachings require a significant amount of work to prepare them for distribution.

This is just a summary of what we do. The ARCHIVE was established with virtually no seed funding and has developed solely through the kindness of many people, some of whom we have mentioned at the front of this book and most of the others on our Web site. We sincerely thank them all.

Our further development similarly depends upon the generosity of those who see the benefit and necessity of this work, and we would be extremely grateful for your help.

The ARCHIVE TRUST has been established to fund the above activities and we hereby appeal to you for your kind support. If you would like to make a contribution to help us with any of the above tasks or to sponsor books for free distribution, please contact us at our Weston address.

The LAMA YESHE WISDOM ARCHIVE is a 501(c)(3) tax-deductible, non-profit corporation dedicated to the welfare of all sentient beings and totally dependent upon your donations for its continued existence.

Thank you so much for your support. You may contribute by mailing a check, bank draft or money order to our Weston address; by making a donation on our secure Web site; by mailing us your credit card number or phoning it in; or by transferring funds directly to our bank—ask us for details.

LAMA YESHE WISDOM ARCHIVE MEMBERSHIP

In order to raise the money we need to employ editors to make available the thousands of hours of teachings mentioned above, we have established a membership plan. Membership costs US$1,000 and its main benefit is that you will be helping make the Lamas' incredible teachings available to a worldwide audience. More direct and tangible benefits to you personally include free Lama Yeshe and Lama Zopa Rinpoche books from the ARCHIVE and Wisdom Publications, a year's subscription to *Mandala*, a year of monthly pujas by the monks and nuns at Kopan Monastery with your personal dedication, and access to an exclusive members-only section of our Web site containing special, unpublished teachings currently unavailable to others. Please see www.LamaYeshe.com for more information.

MONTHLY E-LETTER

Each month we send out a free e-letter containing our latest news and a previously unpublished teaching by Lama Yeshe or Lama Zopa Rinpoche. To see more than fifty back-issues or to subscribe with your email address, please go to our Web site.

THE FOUNDATION FOR THE PRESERVATION OF THE MAHAYANA TRADITION

The Foundation for the Preservation of the Mahayana Tradition (FPMT) is an international organization of Buddhist meditation study and retreat centers, both urban and rural, monasteries, publishing houses, healing centers and other related activities founded in 1975 by Lama Thubten Yeshe and Lama Thubten Zopa Rinpoche. At present, there are more than 145 FPMT activities in over thirty countries worldwide.

The FPMT has been established to facilitate the study and practice of Mahayana Buddhism in general and the Tibetan Gelug tradition, founded in the fifteenth century by the great scholar, yogi and saint, Lama Je Tsongkhapa, in particular.

Every two months, the Foundation publishes a wonderful news journal, *Mandala*, from its International Office in the United States of America. To subscribe or view back issues, please go to the *Mandala* Web site, www.mandalamagazine.org, or contact:

FPMT
1632 SE 11th Avenue, Portland, OR 97214
Telephone (503) 808-1588; Fax (503) 808-1589
info@fpmt.org
www.fpmt.org

The FPMT Web site also offers teachings by His Holiness the Dalai Lama, Lama Yeshe, Lama Zopa Rinpoche and many other highly respected teachers in the tradition, details about the FPMT's educational programs, audio through FPMT radio, a complete listing of FPMT centers all over the world and in your area, a link to the excellent FPMT Store, and links to FPMT centers on the Web, where you will find details of their programs, and to other interesting Buddhist and Tibetan home pages.

Discovering Buddhism at Home
Awakening the limitless potential of your mind,
achieving all peace and happiness

This fourteen-module program is designed as an experiential course in Tibetan Buddhist philosophy and practice. The teachings contained herein are drawn from the Gelug tradition of Lama Tsongkhapa, a great fourteenth century saint and scholar. These teachings come in an unbroken lineage from Shakyamuni Buddha, who first imparted them some 2,600 years ago, since when they have passed directly from teacher to disciple down to the present day.

The realizations of Shakyamuni Buddha cannot be measured but it is said that the Buddha gained direct insight into the nature of reality, perfected the qualities of wisdom, compassion and power, and then revealed the path to accomplish those same realizations to his disciples. The Buddha's teachings have been presented in various ways by different holy beings over the centuries to make them more accessible to those of us who did not have the opportunity to meet the Buddha himself. Lama Tsongkhapa was one such holy being and his teachings on the *lam-rim* (graduated path to enlightenment) are the heart of the Discovering Buddhism at Home program.

In addition, two contemporary masters, Lama Thubten Yeshe (1935–1984), and Lama Zopa Rinpoche (1945–), have imparted these teachings to their students in a deep and experiential way, leading thousands of seekers to discover for themselves the truth of what the Buddha taught. The methods and teachings found in this program also reflect the unique styles of these two great teachers and are meant to help students get an experiential taste of the Buddha's words.

There are two levels of participation that you may choose from when you embark on this program. Within each of the fourteen modules there are discourses, meditations and other practices, readings and assessment questions. As a casual student you may do some or all of the above as you wish. Alternatively, you can engage in this program as a certificate student, in which case you will see on the summary sheet that comes with each module the requirements to be fulfilled. With each module you also receive a Completion Card, which you have to fill out if you want to get a certificate. Although we recommend doing the modules in order, you don't have to.

When you have completed all fourteen cards you can receive the certificate of completion issued by the Education Department of FPMT and the FPMT's spiritual director, Lama Zopa Rinpoche, which simply gives you the satisfaction of having completed a very comprehensive engagement with the path to enlightenment.

Discovering Buddhism at Home is intended to be more than an academic undertaking and if you want to gain some experience of what the Buddha taught you are encouraged to make it a personal goal to fulfill all of the course requirements and thus qualify for the completion certificate, which symbolizes your commitment to spiritual awakening. When you get it you should rejoice deeply, being moved by how your mind has changed in the process.

The Discovering Buddhism at Home package includes the following:
A different Western teacher teaches each module. You will receive these teachings on audio CD (the length of each module varies but there are approximately 4–8 teaching CDs per module). Additionally, you will receive audio CDs of the guided meditations (2–4 CDs per module).

Each module also has a Course Materials text CD containing all the written transcripts of the teachings and meditations in printed form and a text CD containing the Required Reading materials for all fourteen modules (but not the commercially published books, which you have to acquire on your own and are listed under Required and Suggested Reading).

An on-line bulletin board has been created exclusively for Discovering Buddhism at Home participants. When you purchase your first module you will receive instructions on how to join and thus enhance your learning experience through this virtual discussion group.

Each module costs US$40. If you fulfill all the requirements it should take you about two months to complete each one. However, you are free to buy the modules whenever it suits you; when you finish one you can simply buy the next. If you want to receive a completion certificate you will also receive the support of an FPMT elder, who will reply to your answers to the assessment questions to ensure that your understanding is on track with and to guide you through the fourteen modules. You can purchase the modules directly from the FPMT shop at www.fpmt.org/shop or by emailing materials@fpmt.org.

OTHER TEACHINGS OF LAMA YESHE AND LAMA ZOPA RINPOCHE CURRENTLY AVAILABLE

BOOKS PUBLISHED BY WISDOM PUBLICATIONS

Wisdom Energy, by Lama Yeshe and Lama Zopa Rinpoche

Introduction to Tantra, by Lama Yeshe

Transforming Problems, by Lama Zopa Rinpoche

The Door to Satisfaction, by Lama Zopa Rinpoche

Becoming Vajrasattva: The Tantric Path of Purification, by Lama Yeshe

The Bliss of Inner Fire, by Lama Yeshe

Becoming the Compassion Buddha, by Lama Yeshe

Ultimate Healing, by Lama Zopa Rinpoche

Dear Lama Zopa, by Lama Zopa Rinpoche

How to Be Happy, by Lama Zopa Rinpoche (forthcoming)

About Lama Yeshe:

Reincarnation: The Boy Lama, by Vicki Mackenzie

About Lama Zopa Rinpoche:

The Lawudo Lama, by Jamyang Wangmo

You can get more information about and order the above titles at www.wisdompubs.org or call toll free in the USA on 1-800-272-4050.

TRANSCRIPTS, PRACTICES AND OTHER MATERIALS

See the LYWA and FPMT Web sites for transcripts of teachings by Lama Yeshe and Lama Zopa Rinpoche and other practices written or compiled by Lama Zopa Rinpoche.

DVDS OF LAMA ZOPA RINPOCHE

There are many available: see the Store on the FPMT Web site for more information.

What to do with Dharma teachings

The Buddhadharma is the true source of happiness for all sentient beings. Books like the one in your hand show you how to put the teachings into practice and integrate them into your life, whereby you get the happiness you seek. Therefore, anything containing Dharma teachings, the names of your teachers or holy images is more precious than other material objects and should be treated with respect. To avoid creating the karma of not meeting the Dharma again in future lives, please do not put books (or other holy objects) on the floor or underneath other stuff, step over or sit upon them, or use them for mundane purposes such as propping up wobbly tables. They should be kept in a clean, high place, separate from worldly writings, and wrapped in cloth when being carried around. These are but a few considerations.

Should you need to get rid of Dharma materials, they should not be thrown in the rubbish but burned in a special way. Briefly: do not incinerate such materials with other trash, but alone, and as they burn, recite the mantra OM AH HUM. As the smoke rises, visualize that it pervades all of space, carrying the essence of the Dharma to all sentient beings in the six samsaric realms, purifying their minds, alleviating their suffering, and bringing them all happiness, up to and including enlightenment. Some people might find this practice a bit unusual, but it is given according to tradition. Thank you very much.

Dedication

Through the merit created by preparing, reading, thinking about and sharing this book with others, may all teachers of the Dharma live long and healthy lives, may the Dharma spread throughout the infinite reaches of space, and may all sentient beings quickly attain enlightenment.

In whichever realm, country, area or place this book may be, may there be no war, drought, famine, disease, injury, disharmony or unhappiness, may there be only great prosperity, may everything needed be easily obtained, and may all be guided by only perfectly qualified Dharma teachers, enjoy the happiness of Dharma, have love and compassion for all sentient beings, and only benefit and never harm each other.

LAMA THUBTEN ZOPA RINPOCHE was born in Thami, Nepal, in 1945. At the age of three he was recognized as the reincarnation of the Lawudo Lama, who had lived nearby at Lawudo, within sight of Rinpoche's Thami home. Rinpoche's own description of his early years may be found in his book, *The Door to Satisfaction*. At the age of ten, Rinpoche went to Tibet and studied and meditated at Domo Geshe Rinpoche's monastery near Pagri, until the Chinese occupation of Tibet in 1959 forced him to forsake Tibet for the safety of Bhutan. Rinpoche then went to the Tibetan refugee camp at Buxa Duar, West Bengal, India, where he met Lama Yeshe, who became his closest teacher. The Lamas went to Nepal in 1967, and over the next few years built Kopan and Lawudo Monasteries. In 1971 Lama Zopa Rinpoche gave the first of his famous annual lam-rim retreat courses, which continue at Kopan to this day. In 1974, with Lama Yeshe, Rinpoche began traveling the world to teach and establish centers of Dharma. When Lama Yeshe passed away in 1984, Rinpoche took over as spiritual head of the FPMT, which has continued to flourish under his peerless leadership. More details of Rinpoche's life and work may be found in *The Lawudo Lama* and on the LYWA and FPMT Web sites. In addition to several LYWA and FPMT books, Rinpoche's other published teachings include *Wisdom Energy* (with Lama Yeshe), *Transforming Problems, Ultimate Healing, Dear Lama Zopa, How to Be Happy* and many transcripts and practice booklets.

AILSA CAMERON first met Buddhism at Tushita Retreat Centre in India in 1983 and has since been involved in various activities within the FPMT, primarily in relation to the archiving, transcribing and editing of the teachings of Lama Zopa Rinpoche and Lama Yeshe. With Ven. Robina Courtin, she has edited *Transforming Problems* and *The Door to Satisfaction*, by Lama Zopa Rinpoche, and *The Bliss of Inner Fire*, by Lama Yeshe, for Wisdom Publications. She has also edited Rinpoche's *Ultimate Healing* and *How to Be Happy* for Wisdom. After working originally in India and Nepal, she went to Hong Kong in 1989 to help organize the electronic version of the LAMA YESHE WISDOM ARCHIVE. Ordained as a nun by His Holiness the Dalai Lama in 1987, she has been a member of the Chenrezig Nuns' Community in Australia since 1990. She is currently a full time editor with the LAMA YESHE WISDOM ARCHIVE, for whom she has edited many teachings, including *Teachings from the Mani Retreat* and *Teachings from the Vajrasattva Retreat*.